Bricks and Roses

By

Crae F. Hancock

This book is a work of non-fiction. Names and places have been changed to protect the privacy of all individuals. The events and situations are true.

ISBN: 1-4107-8786-9 (e-book)
ISBN: 1-4107-8785-0 (Paperback)

This book is printed on acid free paper.

1stBooks - rev. 02/12/04

TABLE OF CONTENTS

THE GREAT SPIRIT

The Great Spirit is recognized by many Native inhabitants of North America. As far as I can ascertain there is not a religion, no group or support group and there are no buildings, ie. Churches. The Great Spirit does not live in the heavens, on Mt. Olympus or on some other planet. The Great Spirit lives in, exists in, every living thing. The Great Spirit is not God or one of the Gods. It appears that the Great Spirit has been here ever since life began. In a literal sense the Great Spirit is life. The Great Spirit personally directs those who listen. The Great Spirit could be considered to be a positive conscience. The Great Spirit is not gender, neither male or female. It is easy to pray to the Great Spirit because the Great Spirit is in you. The Great Spirit knows all your concerns, worries, and troubles. The Great Spirit also knows when you are happy. Even though I use many biblical scriptures in the text of this book I use the words; "The Great Spirit" instead of the commonly used word; "God". In a few instances I use the word; "Creator" as a synonym for the "Great Spirit". In the Old Testament there is a lot of confusion in regard to the entity God. God is the word interjected in place of the entities found in the original Hebrew writings. Some of these entities were the Canaanite Gods; El, Eljon, Elo, Elohim, Moelec, Melcom and others. All were translated at times into the words "God" and "Lord". The Confusion intensifies when you find that a Hebrew word "Yah" or "Yahveh" is also translated into the words "God" and "Lord". It is very easy to observe which entity the writer of a passage did acknowledge. The writers name tells us in the suffix of the name. For Instance; Daniel, Samuel, Joel etc. I think you can ascertain the "El" suffix. Now look at the names Obadiah, Jonah, Micah, Zepaniah, Isiah, etc. By the suffix of the names you can see "Ah" a form of the Hebrew word "Yah". When translated the Hebrew word "Yah" means "I am" and "Veh" means; "That is". "Yahveh"; "I am that is". It is of interest to note that Moses told the Hebrews not to worship the

Canaanite Gods. It is also notable that at the time of Solomon there was a division amongst the Hebrew tribes. Ten tribes became the Israelites and two tribes became the Judahites. They obviously acknowledged different Gods. Native Indian languages use individual's names to also tell you information about the individual. A Ute Indian name of "Nahcagant" means; seeker of light and brillance. I don't think the name meant that the person liked looking at light bulbs or stars. It could mean that the individual sought and listened to the Great Spirit. By the way, did you happen to see "Ah" in the name? Another unique fact is about the extinct Indian tribe from California called the "Yahi". The last living Yahi was a man named "Ishi". I happened upon a video in the county library that was about the Yahi and Ishi and the circumstances of their extinction. The interesting fact is that in Hebrew a man is called; "Ish". Curious as it is, Ishi could be called a "man" of "Yahi" or "I am". Yah or Yahveh, "I am that is" appears to be a very good synonym for "The Great Spirit".

Be sure that you read my next book. It is called; "Seeking Truth".

PREFACE

Every day of our lives we are confronted by the various and obvious differences, in nature and behavior, between men and women. In this book I won't be talking about the more common and evident observations regarding physical differences. I want to concentrate on the more important differences. These differences are more than just skin deep. Because one can't visualize these differences it takes some time to evaluate them. In order for humans to understand any new facts it helps for a sentence picture to be verbally painted. TV talk show hosts have, in the past, capitalized on some points. They have tried but will never be able to exhaust the subject of the differences between the sexes.

Life likes to abruptly confront us head on with what can be very delicate issues. Most of the time these issues are generated out of the differences between genders. Even though we most often ignore the differences between us there are times when the difference becomes close enough to our perception that ignoring the issues becomes impossible. For that reason, at some point in life, we all will have to personally deal with the differences.

You can ask anyone you know about gender rift and by their response you will see that through the years there have always been different thoughts and theories about the differences between the sexes. Most of these theories and the philosophies that stem from them, after a period of time, usually fade into obscurity. If the thoughts don't die out, they may reach a point of maturity that compels us to investigate them further. For that reason it is no wonder that the books on this subject are as diverse as they are numerous.

In this book it is my intention to try focusing my readers attention to the basic instinctual programs for both male and female. I can then use incidents with which some people may relate and by these situations I can attempt showing the male and female mentality in action. If I can paint a vivid picture with words then I hope that we can stand back and evaluate ourselves and proceed to make some beneficial changes in our lives.

One of the results that occurs from the fact that most of us don't understand the differences between the genders is that many of us fail in any effort to develop a meaningful male-female relationship. We tend to exist in a realm of our life that is way short of what it could be. I am amazed when I think of present day conveniences and compare that thought with the information about life styles only 100 years ago. Humanly, we take for granted our modern conveniences and the reduced workload that they provide.

On this subject I can speak to you from my own experience because in my past I have been deficient in the area of understanding the differences. One of my problems is that I spent way too much time in the rut of modern life. All of our present conveniences, instead of freeing me, gave me more time with which I involved myself with numerous projects, I was "too busy". To busy to take the time needed to

learn. Being intelligent but ignorant about
females and also being a ego-male, I,
mentally, was unable to make any positive
changes in my life in male, female
relationships. Therefore my failings, in
trying to maintain a healthy relationship with
the female gender didn't register, in my
thinking, as a personal problem. Though I was
beginning to realize something was definitely
wrong, I did not know what and, really did not
want to know what, the problem was. So, in my
case, I remained lost in my own ways. There
were no changes in my beliefs or behavior. In
all honesty, after having been dumped a time
or two, my first thoughts were; "What the hell
is wrong with her"! After you have read this
far I'm sure that you are able to observe by
my keen mind set and can see that I definitely
had no ability to understand and comprehend
the nature and needs of women.

Time passing did not cure my problems.
Recognizing something was wrong I wrongly
thought that I knew the answer. I thought that
the whole problem would be solved if a woman
would think and act more like a man. After

all, aren't we all homosapiens, human beings? Don't we all have similar body parts such as arms, legs, eyes, ears and noses? Being so much the same, how could we possibly be so different?

Crazy as it is, even after I suffered a great deal of emotional pain and agony, it was tough for me, an ego male, to admit any fault. With my male ego fully intact it took a long time before I finally concluded that I was wrong. Wrong to think that women should become more like men.

Like some men, I like to fix things. Fixing an item must, somehow, bolster my ego. Even if something is not broken, I like to tinker around with it just to see how it works. I might like to do it for no other reason than to just add my mark to it by, in some fashion, tuning it up. I hope you are beginning to comprehend my man mind. It should be discernable to you that after admitting I was wrong, my next male step was to try and fix or tune up the problem. Contemplating, I thought that I should try and find a repair/tune-up manual on women and men. With the primary concept of fixing my problem I thought that, if it is possible that men and women are different, I should start out by learning about those differences. Hopefully, by educating myself, I could change my way of thinking and maybe that could help me recuperate from my attempts and failings. I began to search and investigate, oh, by the way, mechanical fix it publishers didn't carry a manual on men and women. While searching I found another alarming discovery. I already knew that I didn't understand women, but to my surprise I discovered that I didn't understand myself, i.e. men, either.

The twelve-step program for a recovering alcoholic includes as the initial step that one has to realize and admit that a problem exists. Only then can progress be made in correcting the problem. It is unbelievably simple; "we don't ever fix anything unless it's broken" and even then, we won't fix it until it is absolutely necessary. When we arrive at the point of finally fixing something, the problem and our self are usually in dire need. The pressing situation of recognizing my absolute failure finally caused me to believe and admit to myself that fixing the problem is the only solution. Of Course, during our age of time, instead of fixing a problem our self, we usually attempt hiring a supposed professional. This reminds me of a story I heard about a person driving around town on a flat tire even after a dozen people had told him it was flat. No matter how many people told him, it didn't do any good, because he just did not want to believe it. It seems we all have a hard time admitting to our self one fact and that is that most men and women have trouble understanding the nature of each other. At this point I'm talking to you in more depth than the thoughts; "women like to shop" and men like sports". For myself, by experience, I recognized I had a flat tire, a big problem. I still didn't want to believe that the problem could be myself. I wasn't able to learn anything in that direction until after I made the difficult personal admission, "I've got some problems".

Please don't misconstrue my position in relating this to you. It is not that men are always the problem, nor is it that women are either. The issue is that both male and female don't understand what makes them selves and each other tick and therefore neither sex knows how to deal with the sticky differences between themselves.

I'm not patronizing any religion, but I do believe that spiritual entities or forces exist. For my own reasons I do not call the prime entity "God". Instead, I use the term "Great Spirit". I feel better believing the concept that man must have outside help than I do about believing the opposite, that mankind, along with the rest of life, haphazardly and spontaneously emerged by itself from the muck into being. In my thinking it seems obvious that there must be a Creator and there must have been a plan concerning mankind. Being a builder by trade, I knew that a blueprint comes before any building and that if I have any questions about a particular building, I can get answers from the blueprint. Some of you, who are not builders or who are not involved in building, don't understand the total purpose of a blueprint. Most of you would think that it is just a set of drawings showing the builder how to put the building together, a set of instructions per se. That idea is partially correct, but it is not the main reason for a set of prints. A designer or architect draws a set of prints for the primary purpose of causing the components of the building to come together to see how the components will fit with each other. In prints there is "created", if you will, a model, which must work in conjunction with all the other pieces, parts, fixtures and factors. That way when the building is constructed it will look and work as it was planned to be and not as if it all just happened. I am always amazed when someone wants an addition to an existing building but what they want to add doesn't fit with the existing building. In short, just the idea of the addition won't work all by it's self. What good is a bathroom addition if you can't get the plumbing to drain. It's in the planing stage that these problems are solved. With these ideas in mind I am compelled to believe that there must be a plan for our own lives".

1. TRUTH

If there is a Creator and a plan I sure wanted to find out what that plan is. For you who are reading this, if you admit that there is a presence greater than your self then you should be able to follow along with what I have to say. If you don't believe in anything at all, or you don't want to admit so, then just follow the logic of what I'm saying. I'm a firm believer in logic. Another good word combination that can be exchanged for logic is the word group "common sense". There should be a prerequisite college class called "Common Sense" and another named "Human Nature".

For myself, the intricacies of life make a statement that speaks loud and clear; life is to fragile and complex to have just emerged on it's own. To most of us in an uneducated state, it feels acceptable to believe that something designed us, made the design reality, engineered it's propagation and then coincidentally and simultaneously created all the necessary elements for sustaining itself.

Have you ever thought about the fact that trees inhale carbon dioxide and exhale oxygen and man inhales oxygen and exhales carbon dioxide. Sounds so simple, but it's not simple. Each individual's ability to sustain his or her life is interrelated to other outside forces. All of life is interdependent. We all have needs that are met from outside of our zone of control. These needs, to name a few, are; breathable air, accommodating temperatures, sufficient water, food, sleep, shelter, clothing, minerals, immunities and elemental resistance. Some of these needs may seem controllable by our selves, but when thought of in their extended relation, all are beyond our reach. Of course we think that we can control what we eat, and when we eat it. We don't think about the extension of all the circumstances involved with the function of eating. Ponder the variables that could control what we eat. Things such as rain, wind, temperature, disease, oxygen, carbon dioxide, microorganisms, pollination, insects and etc. not to mention thinking about food processing. Most of the foods we eat must be processed, cooked, or modified for consumption. How do you make the instant that instant potatoes are made from? Just joking. By the way, who made the potato in the first place? Wait a minute, in order to eat we can't forget our body. It might not be hungry when we think it should be. We didn't mention all that is going on inside the body. There are many organs performing different necessary tasks. Inside you there is something going on at all times, 24 hours a day. Some of these body processes necessary for eating are breathing, blood circulation, coordination, chewing, swallowing, and digestion. Digestion depends on special organs for the secretion of acids and further depends on the assistance of microorganisms in order for the stomach to digest properly. Eating and digestion also involves the intestines, the colon, and the circulatory system to transport the digested food to human cells. Finally, eating must have a process for waste elimination. I'm sure that each of you could think of something that I've left out. My point is that something we think is so simple, such as eating, in reality, it's workings are very complex.

Something that we thought that we were in total control of just became something that we can't possibly control all of. With this information you can see that the brain has a difficult job. You have all heard of voluntary and involuntary muscles. At one time I mistakenly thought that breathing was involuntary. It's not. Your brain has to tell your lungs to inhale and exhale. A few years ago I fell from twenty feet at a construction site. I was on top of a scaffold masking off for paint. A person on the floor hollered, "the call is for you" and tossed my cell phone up. I don't remember anything else but I'm told that I caught the phone and then jumped up to a log beam about eight feet away. I successfully made it to the log beam and caught it with my arms but I severely hit my head on it when jumping up from underneath. I must have knocked myself out then because I fell down with my head leading the way. "Cause and effect". Catching the phone on the scaffold was the "cause". The "effect" was that I was in a comma for eight days and in the hospital for two months. My brain was damaged which is called T.B.I., Traumatic

Brain Injury. I fractured my skull, broke a few ribs and broke my right wrist. I was taken by life flight and was flown to the University hospital in Salt Lake where I was in intensive care and was put on life support machines that kept my body functions going because my brain wasn't. When the doctors took me off the life support systems I couldn't breathe. The brain has to tell the lungs to work. Sounds simple but I had to learn, by trial and error, how to breathe again.

Specific Functions

Being acquainted with various tools in the construction trade I am aware of the fact that each tool is designed for a specific task and, more times than not, a particular tool is not suitable for performing a task other than what it was designed for. A router performs all the functions of a router, it can cut wood, but compared to a skill saw it cannot accurately and speedily cross cut a framing stud to length. I'm attempting to communicate to you that all created things are designed for a specific reason or task. Nothing created is capable of doing everything equally as well as every other created thing.

Everything is interdependent.

All things in our realm, organic and inorganic, everything, including our selves, are interdependent. This concept, when accepted, causes you to think about all the intertwined links.

We are designed to be uniquely different.

With the awareness of our interdependency let us move back to the design differences between men and women. Yes, we have been designed to be different. Yet, being different we, by design, are meant to be interdependent. By logical evaluation I knew that this was the case. Constructing buildings, the buildings them selves have similarities, but every part, though different and separate is, by absolute necessity and by design, meant to interface with all other factors of the building. Accepting differences and interdependence as a fact for our selves I definitely wanted to know about myself and about how I was designed to operate. I knew, by instinct and by my failure, I was not operating according to the plan. I felt like a welder tied to a task of medical surgery, which would put me completely out of my element. "Ad lib" does not work in the medical field, in welding, rough framing, in finish carpentry or in any of the building trades.

Finding out the way I should act would not be easy, there appeared to be far to many options and far to many misleading role models. However, the concept is simple, find out how I'm supposed to act and then start acting that way. After that, find out how and why women act the way they do. Find out how they are, by intent and design, supposed to act and then, but not least, find out about and understand the interdependence in the designs for both men and women. Another suitable word adding clarity for interdependence, in this case, would be the word "multi-purpose". Men can do a lot of the tasks that women do and vice-versa. However, it is clear to me, both men and women are designed and are specialized for different purposes.

The Search for the Architect

To address any questions about why a blue print is drawn the way it is one must go to the architect. For information about the blue print for humanity one would need to ask the entity responsible. In this case, for myself, it was obviously The Great Spirit, the creator. Because of my fear of the unknown I was assuredly timid. Do I dare even ask? I was certainly unsure of getting an audience or an answer but I knew that common sense combined with a religious background had taught me that asking would be the place to start. At this point I was wary of interpreters and underlings, I wanted to go right to the prime source. I decided that even if I didn't get an answer I certainly wouldn't be any worse off for having tried. Taking this step reminded me of the dilemma I suffered when having to admit being wrong. Asking somebody else is admitting that you don't know and not knowing makes you feel insecure. Most of us spend much of our lives trying to overcome insecurities of one kind or another. One of the negative ways that we do this is to build a false sense of confidence about our self. Having to admit being wrong and then having to ask direction is a severe blow to the ego, particularly for the male ego.

The Response

After three divorces, mercy and apathy would be appropriate words to describe how the Great Spirit must have felt about me when observing my relationship inability and my lack of knowledge on our subject. Because of my marriage troubles I had confused anguish over my worries and concerns regarding marriage and the opposite sex. With the resulting lack of confidence in myself I didn't think that I would have any return communication from my supplication. I was surprised. I think the fact that I was so pathetic in my misconceptions and in my lack of understanding that sympathy was given for my petition. I received an answer.

No one had ever explained or attempted to explain male - female relationships to me. I'm not talking about kissing, holding hands or any aspect of physical contact. Those are the easy steps. This was not a class that was offered in any of my schooling. Psychology 101, which I took in college, did not come close to the subject. Because I had gone to a church college the class on marriage and children was religiously biased and was lacking in explanation on relationships. It was just taken for granted that when one was ready then a relationship would just fall into place by itself. Instead of teaching information about how to get along in a marriage the class on marriage was geared toward women and was used for prodding them to get married. One of the requirements for these young women was the making or fashioning of a "hope Chest" wherein the hopeful bride to be placed baby socks, receiving blanket, magazine pictures of dream houses, kitchens and a written description of what the hoping girl thought the future husband should be. Instead of addressing any form of reality, most of the hopeful girls described their dream man to be a dark, handsome return missionary, with no thought of all the other characteristics necessary for being a good husband and father. This was definitely a class for women, not for men. After evaluation I never even considered taking the class, and if I had, it would have meant that I would have been the only guy in there. The very idea was completely out of the question.

As I mentioned earlier, I use the word "Great Spirit" to define the designer of life. It is my opinion that the dictionary definition for the word "God" when researched is found to be unsuitable. There may be many God. The word "God", when looked up in Webster's and most other dictionaries is synonymous with the old English word "Gad" and both originally meant, "host, group or troop". Both words had a plural connotation as is similar for the words, "herd and flock", all are plural without the addition of the suffix "s". "God", "Gad", "Gott" and "Goth" meant the pantheon, the whole group of ancient deities (God). I'm not disputing that there very well may be a pantheon of the "God", and

allowing that, I choose to use the word "Great
Spirit". An option that appears viable to me
is that the Great Spirit uses, has used, the
"God" for a purpose and, more likely than not,
created the "God" Himself for that purpose.
The concept seems logical to me that too many
Chiefs and not enough Indians can cause
confusion. Can you imagine more than one Bill
Clinton or more than one of any president at a
time? I don't intend to side track us into the
study of present day religion and its'
etymology from ancient myth and belief.
Though extremely interesting and enlightening
it would definitely be a subject for a book
all on it's own.

You can tell by now that I believe in the
super-natural. That is, I believe in a
difference between the spiritual realm and our
mortal existence and that there can be
communication between the two. Communication
may be telepathic, and can occur as the result
of human worry and stress, both conscious and
subconscious. It can also be the result of
overt and covert meditation. Intentional
meditation of any meaning is preceded and

12

followed by subconscious silent petition. Usually, even us with the dullest of perception, we can see in the face of anyone who is oppressed or distressed, a look that silently communicates to us that same emotional state. Communication between the normal and paranormal is also the result of overt petition, or as the religious call it, "prayer". For myself, in this case, I must have combined all of the above; worry, stress, silent and overt petition. However it was, I don't know, but I do know that I was super-naturally, telepathically,[1] shown a synonymy called *"Bricks and Roses"*. In this analogy between simple, understandable and identify-able subjects symbolizing the complexities of men and women, there was description and reason for the differences between men and women. The differences include different aptitudes, capabilities and different physio-logical and psychological characteristics. For myself, the analogy made the design intent for

---

[1] **Telepathy**, from Websters: supposed communication between minds by some means other than the normal sensory channels; transference of thought.

both of the sexes easier to understand and comprehend.

Our ninety's era of women's rights, liberation and gay life styles has tried to blend the differences between men and women into one character role where one or the other gender is caught playing both male and female parts. Interchanging and adopting of roles causes, for both sexes, a psychological stigma that reverses the traditional male, female roles. Women acting roles of men and men acting like women can be seen in the lives of homosexuals. Even without being homosexual obvious role reversals show up in the lives of many mature adults. Some of these reversals are simple, like the switching of assertiveness, a traditional male pattern for that of submissiveness, a long established female trait.

Like myself, most men today have atrociously failed in their role to be stable, responsible providers and protectors. Men's failure is due in part to societal evolvement wherein the financial demands of marriage and family have continued to steadily increase causing a hopelessness and despondency that is overwhelming to the extent that many men have bailed out. Becoming homeless by choice but being freed from the heavy weight of the financial end of family responsibility. In the animal kingdom we rarely find any species diverting from the necessary, time substantiated role patterns, but then they don't have to pay income tax, balance the bank account, buy cars, pay licenses and insurance, pay all the other bills and work endless hours trying to make ends meet. It's no wonder that at the end of the day most men and women plop down in front of the TV and end up staying there until they go to bed in order to escape the oppressive rigors and demands of modern life. The pressure of modern life causes people to change. Men, instead of being committed partners, forsake their masculinity and choose to avoid being responsible providers. It's much easier to live the various selfish lifestyles and do so without any concern for wives and children. The departure from the roles that men were designed for and are supposed to be, has and does lead to the use of drugs, alcohol, and promiscuity, which then results in or is associated with other dysfunctional behavior. The current state of irresponsibility, instability, and unaccountability of men forces women to fill the vacant masculine protector, provider roles themselves.

As of recent, I have frequently seen a bumper sticker that says; "*The best man for the job is a woman*"! Women have entered the work force in the most unimaginable places, taking jobs along with men in truck driving, construction, laboring and other once normally considered men's jobs. The result of all these societal changes is not yet completely understood. These changes are partially caused by increasing economic demands and by what starts out as, "*keeping up with the Jones's*". It has now become the acceptable and necessary lifestyle where both male and female partners are required to be the breadwinners.

Women, trying to make an income, some by personal choice and others, compelled by circumstance, usually the result of divorce, compete for most every job available. Even though they are half or more of the population they are considered to be a minority, which allows them to get jobs that in the past were not available to them.

According to Genesis, the first book in the bible, the Great Spirit made the woman as a helpmate[2]. Whether the book's version of how and why is myth or fact isn't the point. The point is that by observing long time traditions and current behavior facts, we can see a prevalent characteristic of women, that of being a helper. This characteristic of being a helper definitely works in a woman's behalf for getting a job and successfully fulfilling it's obligations. Don't get me wrong, I'm not against women working. In my opinion having women in the work place is not altogether a bad situation unless the woman has children and is cutting them short of her mothering skills. In this circumstance I feel that taking care of children should be the

---

[2] **Genesis 2:18** [quoted from the TANAKH] "It is not good for man to be alone; I will make a fitting helper for him".

priority responsibility for a woman, before that of working outside the home. Interesting as it is, women have been created with all the necessary physical hardware for not only giving birth to children but for nurturing them in a fashion that men have never and will never master. It is called "mothering". Fathers that attempt to fill the role of a mother do not have the caring and concern necessary. Men don't have the eyes in the back of their heads knowledge that most mothers exhibit. Even if titled, "Mr. Mom", fathers are never able to fill the vacant shoes of a missing mother. Fathers, however, should and do have more care and concern for their own children than the unattached and disinterested workers in childcare facilities. Childcare facilities are a big compromise in quality environment. They are a place where family ties are weakened and children find themselves patterning after other children rather than after mom and dad.

Today there is an alarming growth in the number of what we call single parent families, which, truthfully, are not families at all but are the evidence of what once was, or was supposed to have been, a family. This presses home the reality of what I've been trying to communicate. The woman has been filling a male position of responsibility as provider all day and now must return home to be a part-time mother. For a woman, this must be a stressful and burdensome existence with little relief or reward for such a demanding performance. Her demanding performance must be compared to the burning of a candle from both ends and to the mental state of being stretched to far in both directions at once. This performance is beyond our design intent and signifies a future collapse or failure in some area an area that usually and regrettably ends up being the family and children.

Children of single parent families must now suffer the shortage of not having both parents and also having the remaining parent only part time. More than likely, a child will be forced into a partial role of the absent father or mother themselves, while still being an adolescent. This is an undesirable situation that extends itself to rob the innocent progeny of a normal childhood. Disappointment, disillusion, frustration and anger consciously and subconsciously influence children as they reach maturity and, sadly, during that time, the same has assisted in developing their personality and character, or the lack of the same.

All the problems that I have mentioned concerning fathers and mothers so far can not be helpful but instead causes negative to make an effect on children and get compiled in their lives, causing them further rejection of time accepted male-female roles. Mistrusting traditional male-female roles by a child focuses their anger toward the missing parent's gender because that person wasn't there while the child was growing up when the child needed them the most.

When I mentioned homosexuality earlier, I didn't further explain why I feel there seems to be such an increase in their numbers. I have heard all kinds of statistics stating that anywhere from five to twenty five percent of the population is homosexual. I don't think, and I certainly hope that the numbers aren't that high. Statistics can be misleading, so I can't say what is really accurate. However, I can see by the design of male and female body parts that the Great Spirit didn't intend any of us to be homosexual. Those few individuals with physical body part exceptions are not design flaws, just production errors. For me, I see homosexuality as the result of male-female role dysfunction. Therefore, one is not born a homosexual but, through dysfunction, becomes a homosexual. An argument similar to this can effectively be used against other deviant sexual behaviors. Some simple, such as excessive masturbation, interest in and use of pornography and other dysfunctional behaviors which are appalling. Such as the practice of bestiality for both men and women, all of which must initially result from inability and failure in traditional male-female role pattern behavior. Deviant sexual behavior, the same as drug and alcohol addiction, is an outward expression of an inward problem.

The breakdown in our family structures leaves the door wide open for alternate lifestyles. I know a lady who is a single parent. Her son is about seven years old. He exhibits a strong need to identify and be accepted by a male figure. His mother is religious and tries living according to religion's principles. She loves her son and takes good care of him. Even with all these positives in place her son still shows that he is lacking the presence of a male role model. At times he doesn't know how to act. He doesn't want to act like his mother, he knows that she is a woman, but he doesn't have a father to pattern after, so he is easily influenced by other boys in child care and school. We can't isolate our children from the world but we can and do influence them by setting the examples that they follow. I have spent some time with this boy and have taken him fishing and played ball with him. He loves it. When he sees me, he runs up to me and gives me a big hug, grabs my hand and walks with me. He is hungry for the companionship of a father figure. I can imagine what it would be like if this need went completely empty and unfulfilled. It would make him that much more susceptible to be drawn towards any male person who, because of homosexual dysfunction, would give him the attention that he craves. This would result in a relationship upon which the homosexual would pray. This relationship if not rejected, would cause homosexual behavior in the child merely as a result of the positive-negative responsive mental conditioning. This still doesn't mean that he would end up being a homosexual. He could go the other way and become like another of my acquaintances' son, who, as a child missed having any relationship with his father. The young man, now as an adolescent, is living a promiscuous lifestyle with sexual contact with many women. He appears to be treating them according to the example and the light in which he sees his mother or is trying to use/abuse them as a result of the anger for his mother leaving his father. Possibly he is trying to fill the empty spot that was left by the absence of his father. Another problem is that Radio and TV are a poor substitute for a genuine parent figure. Both have taught young men that a to be real man, one must be a stud and make all the women one can.

Young girls exhibit similar needs for proper parent role models. Girls who haven't known a healthy father figure seem hungry for that need to be filled. It makes them eager in their youth to catch the attention of a boy. Many of them end up pregnant or with abortions, not because they wanted sex but just because that was the price to pay for the love they never received. They end up with less than is acceptable by trying to fill the void in their life caused by an absent father. A lot of times they will end up rejecting, mistrusting and hating men altogether or they can go the other direction and be helplessly drawn into empty, short term relationships, with men that are going to use them and then leave them.

The problems that are mentioned in this introduction are a result of the breakdown of our families. Contrary to popular opinion, single parenting is not a viable option. It is just the devastating result of a dysfunctional society in which children are compelled to suffer the dysfunction of their parents. The increasing numbers of people living single lives increases homosexuality for both sexes and the inability of both to have genuine lasting male-female relationships.

Wrong behavior loves the opportunity that we provide it. It seems to have an audible voice that says to the child "oh you poor thing, you're hurt and you can't trust anyone, you feel like no one loves you". "I will protect you. Just avoid the opposite sex, drink, do drugs, party or try an alternative lifestyle, then you'll feel better". Rather than try to work out what may be uneasy but what is correct, just bail out and do whatever. Go where the wind blows you. Follow any urge. Certainly, to some dysfunctional person, masturbating or having sex with some other dysfunctional person is much easier than copulation with a wife who is upset and reasonably, won't let you touch her until she feels secure and stable.

As I grew up, I think that I felt the temptations that led toward deviant behaviors.

Temptations that result from the impact of fear and inability generated by the problems that I've mentioned. My most devastating moments occurred when being confronted in stressful male-female relationships, mainly when a woman needed attention, comforting and reassuring and then, in those situations, just plain, not knowing how to act as a healthy, normal, man. I had no idea of how to treat, love or interact with women. If a woman felt insecure, rather than comfort her and build confidence, in her, myself and in our relationship, my comments and actions would further increase her insecurity.

In contradistinction for situations presented herein where a child did not have a father, due to divorce and abandonment, my father was not absent during my childhood. He was there, but he was severely dysfunctional in his male-female relationship with my mother and also his father-child relationships with all of his five children. As a result he was not and could not be a proper father-male role figure. Thank goodness he didn't spend much of his time with us children. He used his hobbies as an escape from his relationship inability. Sometimes, when he was around, out of his inability, he became emotionally and physically abusive. For me, a worse situation than that of not having a father was that of having one that was unsuitable. Many times, because of his behavior, I swore that I would never be like him. I found, to my dismay, in many instances, I acted just like he did. The behavior that he left as an example for me could do nothing but lead me in the wrong direction. I don't want to sound super critical so I do need to say that my father did teach me some valuable lessons. He taught me what I thought was honesty and he expected me to work hard. When I found myself acting dysfunctional in male-female relationships I used him as my excuse to justify the way that I was. It was clear to me that something was wrong so I either blamed him or blamed the other person. The truth was that I didn't function right. Instead of doing something about it I just shrugged it off. With him as a father figure it was easy shrugging off any responsibility to be healthy and normal for the sake of a family. In the sixties and seventies you could get away with being just about any way that you wanted. Every time one turned around someone was doing something that had once been seen as wrong but now appeared to be the new and acceptable way to go about.

As a result of my divorces and the subsequent loss of a relationship with five children I logically determined for myself that there is some way better than the way that I knew. The Great Spirit designed a better way and He intended for me to know about it. A way which doesn't take away our individuality but does, by following it, protect us, help us, give us understanding of the opposite sex and allows us fulfillment in our life. Nothing is happier and causes those surrounding it to be happy than something that performs as intended and keeps on doing it, whether man or machine. Nothing works to it's optimum except that all of it's parts are in order, in good repair and that it's environment is suitably protected for operation. I continue to be baffled by this fact. My transportation, whether car or truck, always seems to run better when it is clean. If this is so, then maybe I should apply the same "clean" condition to myself and to my own procedures. I don't just mean being externally clean in a physical sense but also being psychologically and emotionally clean. Dumping out the garbage of past dysfunctional behavior and getting rid of the old baggage of wrong examples and concepts certainly would be my first places to start cleaning up.

In writing the pages that follow I try, as best as I'm able, to put the ideas shown to me into visual word picture analogies that can convey those concepts and enable others to see them. Some may find that there are repetitious statements. They are allowed because learning is enhanced by repetition. This occurs in three ways. One way is seeing. That is why analogies in the form of word pictures are so important. Second is hearing. The vocal repetition of what one sees. Many times reading out loud to yourself or to another person helps retain the information that you have read. Third is speaking. Telling and discussing with someone about what one has read, seen and heard, which again is repeating it. This solidifies the information and makes it available for recall. If you can use all six senses then you create in yourself what people call photogenic memory. Good speakers have a habit of reiterating certain words or key lines of what they are trying to put across. It is like typing something, emphasizing it by bold print and then, also, underlining it.

The Brick & The Rose

The steps that led me to be aware of the concept that men should be like bricks and women like roses came about as a result of inner struggle with myself. To myself, it was an accepted fact that the Great Spirit or some dispatched spiritual entity, other than my subconscious mind, had begun to show me and restore in me behavior that should have been there if I had not been so messed up and misled. We can all blame our personal problems on a myriad of excuses but in reality those excuses don't hold water. They certainly don't help us deal with and overcome the problems that we are so intent on blaming on others. Never facing our problems means never being able to see and fix those problems. When we have been shown and accept the truth, then there is no longer any excuse. When you get to the point of confronting yourself please realize that there are no time out slips and no doctor releases available. Of course only the Great Spirit can accurately judge our heart, and seems willing to assist those seeking help who are without intent to use it for wrong.

In contrast to the religious theory of future judgement "cause and effect" efficiently deals in a natural way with wrong behavior and with your self. Cause and effect will imminently destroy dysfunction in both man and machine. Hence we have the common used saying of, "he's hell bent on self destruction". This only means that cause and effect is in the process of dealing with a situation. Those who use truth for evil will at some point be facing the discipline of "cause and effect". Some religions call this natural factor "judgement". In any case "cause and effect" happens to anyone who fails to recognize fundamental truth and live by it. No matter what you call it, whether "judgement" or "cause and effect", the outcome is the same for those who reject simple truths. Truth, such as the fact that when one has promiscuous sex with many partners, he will, at some point, end up with one or more of many venereal diseases. Further, "cause and effect" insures that with the same situation, emotional distress for both parties will, whether recognized or not, be linked to such activity.

It is my opinion that truth is not caused by or derived from religion. Religion does however seem to plagiarize on it and then, by doing so, claim some divine authority. The truth is that fundamental truth exists with or without religion. It has existed and will continue to exist perpetually.

There may be many ways to get to Boston. A simple understanding of that fact is a basic truth. It is not my intent to try and convince you that there is only one "right way" to get there. What I am trying to convince you to do is to become a seeker of truth. Truth is not something that once you have some, you can stick it in a jar, put a lid on it and keep it unspoiled. One needs to continually seek truth and add to it the new truth that one learns. This causes you to throw out many things that, at one time, you considered to be truth and replace it with what you have most recently found to be true. Truth needs to be continually purged by it's own self.

It amazes me that most people, including myself, have an innate ability to comprehend fundamental truth. The amazing part is that, although comprehending it, we choose to ignore it and continue on as if we never knew it in the first place. It is no wonder that we, ourselves, by our choices, ignore truth and allow "cause and effect" to eat our lunch on a regular basis.

It seems that when we get to a certain place in our life, the point where we begin pointing our finger in instead of pointing it out. The Great Spirit, or some dispatched paranormal entity such as an "Angel" or "good spirit", is willing and able to fix us, restore us and take us out of our rut of dysfunction. Something happens that on paper may be conceived as figurative but as it effects us it is real and life changing. Religion again tries to capitalize on the intervention of spiritual help and say "it's Jesus who sets you free". It's not Jesus at all that is doing it. It is "truth that sets you free". "Truth" has long been associated with "light". In a sense we are unable to see ourselves, that is, we are unable to recognize our negative behavior. Truth sheds light on the dark area of our behavior. With that light we can clearly see ourselves. The reality of who we really are, when we finally see it, slaps us into awareness. Then truth, synonymous with knowledge, is able to set us free from our past undesirable behavior. Truth is so important that Gods are thought to be associated with or in charge of it.[3] Truth does not force us to accept it and then be modified. We can ignore the truth and continue to stay in our habitual ways, or after a brief attempt at changing, we can give up and slide right back into our old ways. It's our choice. We can spit in the face of opportunity and end up like the biblical Israelites did, forty years in the desert, having never set a foot in the land that they were promised. Or we can accept fundamental truth and decide to permit changes in our behavior because of it.

Obedience is a key word in regard for truth. Failure to be obedient to truth opens

---

[3] **Isaiah 55:16** "...will do so by the God of truth".."will swear by the God of truth"

the door to "cause and effect". For the Israelites, obedience was their key to be able to enter the promise land. However, they never were able to go in because of their personal choice to be disobedient and stay in the rut of their old ways. They failed to be obedient to simple "truth". The result was they had to face the "effect" of their choices. This was a difficult but valuable lesson.

I get tired of listening to the recent word faith preacher teachers. The name it and claim it boys who tout; "Ask", "believe and receive". They gather many adherents by promising the moon if one will just "believe". Further, they try to capitalize and claim responsibility for the future outcome of natural "cause and effect" or they claim healing power when one experience's a natural, spontaneous, adrenaline rush brought on as a result of preacher hype and charisma. Like many of us, these preachers and their hopeful listeners are missing the whole picture. You can't take the tires off of your car and still expect it to go somewhere, no matter how hard you try to "believe" that you can. I think that we need to recognize that we are not video game power players who are in charge of controlling our and other people's lives by moving the joystick of "believing", "meditating", "chanting", "spells" or by other manipulative ways. We can't, by "naming and claiming", enact any super-natural powers and thereby, deviously control and manipulate the Great Spirit to assist us in controlling our environment and the people around us. It appears to me that the Great Spirit is not governed by our whims. He gives and takes as He pleases according to His profound perspective. Why one person can petition and receive an answer and insight and another, ask and not receive anything is beyond my understanding except that it is reasonable to accept the fact that it is not our decision. My point is this: You can try asking and believing until your lips fall off and your brain shorts out. It doesn't mean that you will get help or answers, particularly if your mind desires answers and assistance for malicious intent of some kind. Malicious intent such as using information for controlling others. The Great Spirit doesn't appear to do what is wrong. Therefore, He is not going to give you the positive reinforcement of help and answers when there is any kind of associated negative behavior on your part.

Some of us, again I'm including myself, try to get by with performing according to only a portion of what we have conceived as being right. Because many people are familiar with the bible I'll use an example of this behavior in the biblical story of Saul. According to the story, he was told to go and destroy the Amalakites. He was told not to leave anything alive and not to take any spoils. If you know the story, Saul came back from the battle with a little extra baggage. He had Agag, their king, and the best of their cattle and sheep. Saul, when confronted, denied doing anything wrong. The prophet and according to the story, "God", of course, could hear the livestock bleating and mooing in the background. Saul, when questioned as to why he had not followed the directives, came up with a real good excuse; he saved the animals and was going to offer them up as a sacrifice. I don't really believe the excuse. He probably meant to keep them for himself, but now that he was caught, he tried to smooth over the situation by making the offering. Sounds good, right? Samuel, the prophet, told him something that is indelibly burnt into my mind. "To obey is better than to sacrifice". To obey is better than any excuse that we can come up with not to obey. You can read about it in 1 Samuel 15. Because Saul did not obey, his kingdom and reign was taken from him, the result of "cause and effect". If we don't obey fundamental truth directives then we won't be able to benefit and what's worse, at some point we will have to suffer "the effect".

I did not want to be like the Israelites and end up in the desert of dysfunction for the rest of my life. I knew that I didn't have all of my apples in the basket and that some of the ones that were in there were rotten and had to be removed. So, I moaned, fretted and consciously and subconsciously petitioned for spiritual help. Please help! Tip me upside down and, if you have to, shake me up until all of my junk falls out. Things began to happen, as best as I can explain it, truth began to confront me and I didn't like it. It wasn't fun. Seeing how wrong you are, in my case, made me want to cry, to give up. When I began to recognize and admit wrong choices and bad behavior, I thought that I was hopeless and would never be able to change.

Change is difficult and traumatizing for all of us. It was one of the biggest problems that the Israelites had. They had themselves messed up with their deviant ways and bad behavior. They were told that they would have to change. They weren't expected to do it by themselves. They were given Moses and Aaron as direct spokesmen. They were set free from bondage. More than once, divine intervention saved their bacon. They were supernaturally fed. They were separated from past environment, something necessary for changing ones ways. They were directed by day and by night. They were given rules and guidelines. They had help except that they, themselves, had to choose to use it. Everything was done except do it for them. It's the same for each of us. With all the knowledge and understanding we have, changing our self is still surrounded with all our fears. Fear of many unknowns. Fear is an enemy that keeps us from changing. If we succumb to the fear we end up locked in our past. The very past that we want to be free from.

Being obedient to truth is an investment with a great return. We all would be fools not to recognize it but some how the word hangs ominously over us like some kind of a threat. We don't work well when we feel that we are being forced and threatened. What helps me is looking at it in a different light. Truth is doing me a favor by letting me obey it and, after all, truth is for my own well being.

Trust is another key element. We can't obey what we don't trust. Once we understand the truth then we have to put our trust into it. Then and only then can we even begin to change. This was the beginning of being able to put my trust in anything. As I allowed truth to work on me, it did. I didn't initially enjoy seeing myself through the eyes of truth. It was only after seeing my errors and admitting them that I was pleased with the results.

Even though I had petitioned for spiritual help, It didn't mean that I was ready to receive it. The Great Spirit doesn't move in on your territory until after you've invited Him there and then once there, you are ready to allow Him to assist. He will wait until you are ready, which may be a long time. He's got forever, you don't. Don't get me wrong, the Great Spirit is totally capable of getting to you right now and in such a way that you think that you are the one making the decisions. The tactics that He uses cause you to make a decision for yourself. For example take another story from the bible, that of Jonah and the whale. For instance; Jonah, once he was inside the whale, all by himself, had a drastic change of heart. All of a sudden he really wanted to go to Ninevah. Did the Great Spirit make him change his mind? No, he changed it himself. The Great Spirit just provided him with the opportunity that prompted him to change it. That is part of the paradox that confronts you when your are finding out truth about yourself. Once you recognize the truth, know it and accept it, you still have to make the choice to use it and in order to be able to use it you have to give up something. That something is your old way. The paradox is that you can't be changed until you give up what needs to be changed.

In a sense then, as much as I allowed it, truth worked on changing me. The part of truth that made the most effect on me wasn't the knowledge of knowing something new that I hadn't known before, it was that knowledge of knowing myself by seeing the truth of who and why I was the unacceptable me. Recognizing and being confronted with the real me was shocking and appalling enough to make me want to change. Everyone has, at one time or another, told a lie, and most of us either stretch or omit portions of the truth on a regular basis, but no one sees themselves as a liar because they rationalize their behavior in order to continue the same. If you were slapped up the side of the head with the vivid reality that you are a liar, each time you exaggerated, omitted or out and out lied, and were not able to rationalize it, you would, hopefully, want to modify your behavior and stop doing it. This confrontation doesn't happen until you see yourself in a spiritual light, which is different than how you've ever looked at yourself. Now, observing, you don't even look the same, you're decrepit and ugly, sinister in a way. After seeing myself in that light, I definitely had a big "want to" for making some changes.

When a person wants to get a job they go and make applications and attend interviews. They get the job based on their ability and desire to do the job. Basically one gets the job by presenting that they can and will do what they are asked and told to do. How many of you would hire someone for a job if they told you that they were not going to do what you asked them to do. Instead they would do just what and how they wanted. I don't think so!

The keywords necessary for change are: #1. Truth #2. Trust #3. Recognition #4.

Obedience. Trust and obedience are acts of submission. Submission is a word that feels similar to the word obedience in that we can't stand the idea of being told to do something, whether we want to do it or not. Rest assured that both words describe the avenue by which truth is able to change you. Submission is easier once we first establish trust. Obedience is possible once we have submitted to what we determine we can trust.

In the New Testament Paul asked to be searched for any iniquity that was in him. This was a definite act of submission. What he was submitting to was the concept that he, more likely than not, had some iniquity that needed to be dealt with. Recognizing the concept of possible personal flaws opens the door for supernatural intervention. Even though Paul was not able, at that point, to identify any specifics, he was open for the superior intelligence, power and ability of the Great Spirit to see and expose to him his own faults. This position of recognizing truth, wanting to trust and submitting myself to be obedient to truth was the place in my life that I had come to. Here, at this point, by supernatural means, I began to see my iniquity. Truth can be abrupt and can also be a gentleman. Some how, I didn't just see that I was wrong but I was kindly shown how and why I was wrong. Then great lengths were taken to teach and explain for my understanding the way that I was designed to be and that I should be. This happening was unmerited on my part, other than I was submitting to the truth and wanting to be obedient to what I had found out. As I think of that period of time, it still humbles me and brings tears to my eyes, knowing what a creep I had been and now how undeserving that I was and still am.

3. THE FOUNDATION

Men are often referred to as rocks, Rocky Stallone the stone, block head and so on. There's even a news commentator whose first name is "Stone". In the New Testament J.C. was called a rock and a cornerstone. The Great Spirit is referred to as a rock in both first and second Samuel and again in more than twenty eight passages from the book of Psalms. Peter was also called a rock. When I'm thinking of these examples of men referred to as rocks or stones I don't picture them as round lumpy rocks sitting useless on the ground. I see them, instead, as stones with a purpose, hewn with squared and paralleled sides upon which weight can be evenly distributed. Rock solid, like men with solid character. Such men, solid, with purpose and responsibility, would be good examples for consideration as role models in our own lives. No building remains and suitably exists except that it is built upon a solid foundation. Years ago foundations were not made of poured cement like they are today. They were made of hewn and stacked stone. Many famous writers, when talking of men of character, equate the same with common used colloquialisms like; "solid like a rock", "rock solid", "built like a brick" and "tough as stone". The interpretation I get is that men should be solid and should stand with solid footing. They need to be able to be relied on, counted on and rested on. I think this is why I was given the analogy that a man should be like a brick. A brick is a man made form with use and characteristics similar to that of stone.

By itself a brick doesn't amount to much but when it is fit together with other bricks it becomes an integral part of a whole structure. In the position of being fitted together with other bricks a single brick is able to bear weight many times over its own. However, no brick can carry this load without the help of all the others and without being placed on a solid and strong foundation. Our solid foundation must be truth. Everything rests on truth. The Great Spirit wants men to be more like him self which, of course, would be, in the figurative sense, being like a rock. A rock is solid, supportive and responsible. Much different than what the men of today's society are. Without knowing truth and having a foundation of truth, men, of present, are like broken bricks. They are useless, in a state of disorder and confusion, unable to fulfill the function that they were initially designed for. Am I saying something?

As it says in the book of Genesis, "in the beginning the world was created". I felt, that if this was truly the beginning of things, then, it should be a good place to look for information to support what I was being shown about men and women. In Genesis there is found an explanation of creation. Not an explanation of just the creation of the earth and the heavens but also of the man and woman. The man was supposedly made in the image of the Creator.[4] It makes logical sense

---

[4] **Gen 1:26-27** "God said, "Let us make man in our own image, in the likeness of ourselves, and let them be masters of the fish of the sea, the birds of heaven, the cattle, all the wild animals and all the creatures that creep along the ground". God created man in the image of himself, in the image of God he created him, male and female he created them".

to realize that the Creator did not necessarily make man an exact duplicate of himself in a strict physical sense but more probably made him to be a likeness of his nature and attributes. In Numbers 23:19[5] and in Job 9:32[6] it says about the Great Spirit "He is not a man". He doesn't think like a man. No matter what religion tells us or how much we would like to think that we are made completely in the image of the Great Spirit. These scriptures, along with common sense, tell us differently. Some religions teach that you can become a God. One religion, in particular, teaches that the Great Spirit was once a man himself. In Christianity there are some religions whose teachings depart from the most general interpretation of bible scripture. The other religions, claiming to adhere to the general interpretation, call those that don't adhere to their ideas, a "Cult". However, interestingly enough, Judaism, not believing at all in the New

---

[5]**Numbers 23:19** "God is not a man that He should lie" [in the New Jerusalem translation: "God is not a human being..".]
[6]**Job 9:32** "For He is not a man as I am that I may answer Him,..". [NJV] "For He is not human like me..".

Testament, is not called a "Cult". Still the same, to those who are Jews and to most other theological Christians who adhere to biblical teaching, the notion that the Great Spirit was once a man or that He could have been at anytime anything other than who He is, is called blasphemy and heresy. If the Great Spirit is Alpha and Omega, if He is, as Moses said, "I am", then, in my mind, He couldn't be, the great, "I was". It feels solid to me to think of Him as having been, is and always will be the Great Spirit. In Isaiah 55:8,9[7] it says that the ways and thoughts of the Great Spirit are not as ours but are higher, or above that of ours. Insinuating, again, that the Great Spirit is not a "man". In that regard, by learning truth about myself and by recognizing how pathetic I am, I say, "It's a damn good thing He's not a man"!

By the Genesis account, it is plain for me to see that man did not pre-exist, nor he transported here from some other planet or

---

[7] **Isaiah 55:8,9** "For my thoughts are not your thoughts, neither are your ways my ways", declares the Lord. As the heavens are higher than the earth, so are my ways are higher than your ways and my thoughts than your thoughts".

realm. According to the story, he was created here on the earth and was formed from earth's elements. Genesis 2:7 says that man was formed from the dust of the earth. What becomes of dust mixed with a little water? It becomes mud or clay. With this thought in mind it was easy for me to accept the analogy that a man is like a brick. Men and bricks are both formed from the elements of the earth, pressed into shape, fired, heated and in the case of man, caused to be alive by a process designed by an entity more intelligent than that of the man which is being made. Man, like a brick, is molded and shaped for a special reason, just as a Potter has a purpose in mind when he molds clay into a particular shape or vessel.[8]

Every once in a while I hear people talking with each other about a young child using some commonly heard colloquial phrases such as; "Look at that kid", "what a chunk", "my, my, he's just like a little brick", "boy

---

[8] **Rom 9:20,21** "But who are you, o man, to talk back to God? Shall what is formed say to him who formed it, "Why did you make me like this"? Does not the potter have the right to make out of the same lump of clay some pottery for noble purposes and some for common use?

oh boy, he's sure a chip off the old block". These phrases ultimately mean that the child resembles his father and his father, in some way, apparently, resembles a block or brick.

The Great Spirit didn't just have one brick in mind when He made Adam. He also created reproduction, the avenue by which all men would subsequently be created. Like a factory produces many brick once the mold and mechanism is set. The Great Spirit mechanism of reproduction continues to produce mankind.

The qualities and characteristics for defining both men and brick have many similarities. A little humor, but blockheadedness is a characteristic that the Great Spirit purposefully chose for men. Dependability and integrity are also characteristics that men should have, which are in common with the same characteristics that are necessary for bricks. Compared to women, men, like bricks, have a few rough edges and an unmistakable density. What a good thing it was for me to find out that these characteristics were all part of a plan.

The characteristics of strength, uniformity, dependability, integrity, durability and ability to support all benefit a man just as they benefit bricks when used as part of the structure of a building.

According to the biblical account of Genesis, after the Great Spirit made the man and breathed life into him, He gave him the unique opportunity to walk and talk with Him. During that period of time I'm sure that the Great Spirit filled the man in as to what his function and purpose were. Some helpful insight about service to the Great Spirit is also described in Romans chapter 12. I'm not going to footnote or quote it, but instead I encourage you to take the time to look it up and read it for yourselves.

In Genesis the man is called a caretaker.[9] He was told to have dominion over the animals and to name them. Sounds a lot like

---

[9] **Gen 2:15** [NJV] "Yahweh God took the man and settled him in the garden of Eden to cultivate and take care of it..".
[NIV] "The Lord God took the man and put him in the Garden of Eden to work it and take care of it,..".

responsibility to me. So, man is supposed to take care of everything, which logically includes protecting, providing, accounting, being in charge of and being responsible for. These are all things that describe what a man is supposed to do, even today. There are also those things that man is not supposed to do. If man is to be like a brick he's not supposed to get blown away by the wind of troubles that comes along. He's not to dissolve in the rain of discomfort and not to crumble when the weight of responsibility is piled high upon him. These are all analogous, but I'm sure that you can get the drift of what I'm saying.

According to the story, when the Great Spirit was finished with creating the world and all that was in it, He declared that all that He had done was good, except, it was not good for man to be alone.[10] Is, as it appears here, the creation of a woman an after thought? Was it the result of a dilemma? No, I don't think so. It appears to me that the

---

[10] **Gen 2:18** [NJV] Yahweh God said, "It is not right that the man should be alone, I shall make him a helper".
[NIV] The Lord God said, "It is not good for man to be alone, I will make a helper suitable for him".

Great Spirit always has a plan. His plan is for all things to work well together so, what better way for man not to be alone than for a helpmate, a friend and a partner to be made for the man. A question comes to mind. Why did the Great Spirit make her out of the man rather than make her from the dust as He had done with the man? The reason must be because He perceives every aspect of all things. His choice is the product of good thinking. If He made her from part of the man, that is, took away from the man that which became the woman, then the man will always feel an innate need for her. The man would always want back the part of himself that was removed. It is the part of him that, since that time, is and continues to be, missing. It seems that the Great Spirit does many things at once, or better put, His acts encircle many diverse aspects. One of the results of His multi-facetted ability is that the act of creating mankind as described both affects the woman and benefits the man. Because the woman was part of the man, she will always desire him. She will desire that from whence she came. By the fact that she was taken out of the man we can deduct that whatever the man was before she was taken out is now, at least in part, that which she became. This attempt to define the creation of men and women aligns with both Jewish and Christian theology. Both define the Great Spirit as being both male and female in psyche. This helps one to understand that the Great Spirit is all things by and in him self. This theology is not believed by some religions such as Mormonism. They believe that "God" needs to have a woman or many women in order to create spirit offspring. In Christianity, Judaism and many other religions, the Great Spirit does not need a female counter part, but instead, creates life spontaneously, at will, by just thinking or speaking life into being, therefore, having no need for a female partner involving a sexual act for creating life. In the most widely accepted concept of the Great Spirit likeness, He would be defined to be more like the first man Adam. He would be like Adam was before he was separated into both female and male form. Certainly, if the Genesis account is correct, Adam under went surgery after the fact of his being created in the image of the Great

Spirit. None the less, other variations of the account could still be true when it is said that man was created in "our" image, in the image of the Great Spirit. I suppose that you have a question at this point as to why one puts a plural form "s" at the end of the word God. The reason is that the Genesis account has within it both versions of the creation of man. One stating that "I" created man in my own image" and the other stating "We" created man in *our* image". Which is it? It can't be both. It has to be one or none of the above.[11] The answer to my question is found in the study of the Masoretic texts of the Old Testament. Of recent, scholars have concluded that at least two separate source texts were compiled to make the one text. The first text is called the "Y" source and the second is called the "E" source. "Y" having reference for the singular Hebrew deity known as, "Yahveh". He is the deity who was accepted and worshiped by two Hebrew tribes under the

---

[11] **Genesis 1:26** [NJV] "God said,'Let us make man in our own image, in the likeness of ourselves..".
Genesis 1:27 [NJV] "God created man in the image of himself, in the image of God he created him, male and female he created them"

leadership of Rehoboam. They became known as the house of Judah. The second Old Testament text source is the "E" source, which refers to the plural deity known as "Elohim". This is the pantheon of Canaanite deities worshiped and accepted by the remaining ten tribes under the leadership of Jeroboam. They came to be known as the house of Israel. The split between the Hebrews occurred right after King Solomon died and was the result of Solomon's infidelity to "Y" or "Yahveh". Solomon, in addition to building the Hebrew temple, married pagan women and built and worshiped the "Elohim" [pantheon of El or Eloi] in those pagan temples.[12]

My point, before I became side tracked on biblical texts, is that the Great Spirit can love us like a mother and at the same time be able to discipline us like a father. The Great Spirit is all things in him self and by himself. In the same way Adam, who was made in the Great Spirit likeness, existed before Eve and was, at first, "Adam" all by himself, that is before he under went surgery. After

---

[12] **See 2 Chronicles 10,11 and 12**

surgery Adam is no longer the Adam he was but, by the taking of a rib, he has been split into becoming two persons; "Adam and Eve". Together but separate. The both of them are still "Adam" even after the fact. Interesting as it is, the word "Adam" means "mankind". Don't worry, it's not like the story of Humpty Dumpty Illustration # 3

who, after taking a fall, can not be put back together again. In this case, according to the account in Genesis, the Great Spirit puts Adam back together again by causing the two gender parts of mankind to join together in a form of oneness. Genesis 2:24; "For this reason a man shall leave his father and mother and shall cleave unto his wife and the two shall become one, even one flesh". The word picture I want to paint is that man was initially complete within himself and then after he lost a figurative rib, in order for man to be complete, he must have with him his counterpart, the woman.

When we look at and digest the preceding information, it should begin to make it easy for us to understand why men and women are not alike and why we are not able to always understand each other as well as we would like. In more ways than one, there are certainly differences in the two genders. The part of the man that could understand the woman is missing. It is the part that became his wife. She doesn't really understand him either because she's the part of him that was removed and is no longer part of him. This is a good reason why we need to grasp an understanding of both parts, male and female. Only then can we understand, appreciate and respect each other.

It wouldn't have made any sense for the Great Spirit to make both the man and the woman the same. One does not need two dust pans to clean a floor. You need a broom and a dustpan. The Great Spirit made both the man and the woman with some similarities, one of which is an inborn need and desire for Him. All humanity has a long history of belief in some sort of supernatural being. I would say that it is only through the help of the Great Spirit that we can begin to understand each other. Biblical scripture says that one strand of a rope can be easily broken. Two strands are strong but three strands of a rope cannot be broken (Ecclesiastes 4:12). Each man and each woman needs to have the assistance of that third strand of the rope in order to sustain a viable relationship. Relationships without that third strand can be only as strong as two strands. As such, their partnership is strong but can still be broken. Having truth in ones life can make the difference between having a solid marriage and getting a divorce. It appears to me that the Great Spirit is big on parables. To help me understand women He began to show me that a woman is like a rose. Along with giving me understanding He wanted me to be able to comprehend the magnitude of what His gift to Adam was, the woman, for all mankind (Adam).

A priceless gift for a loving friend is given the utmost care and is received with the same care. It is never to be laid aside or neglected of thought. The rose has long been such a gift. It is a token of esteem and respect and is admired for it's beauty and it's fragrance. It is handled with care and is nourished to last as long as is possible. The cut rose will die but its' life's essence, while present, is kept timeless in memory. Memory of the emotion, love and the thought of the event that brought it's presence as a gift. Such a priceless gift, beyond mere words, did the Creator of life present to Adam the first man.

Like a Rose beautifies its surroundings a woman beautifies her surroundings. She's like a crown on the head of her husband (Proverbs 12:4). The characteristics of a woman can be so well seen in the analogy of a rose. The silky, soft petals are folded tightly around a budded center and are tender and easily damaged. The vulnerability of her beauty is often mistaken for weakness but the truth is; she has such great inner strength that, even though damaged in a tremendous storm, she can endure it. Roses, so vulnerable, beautiful and precious are on the other hand are very hardy.

Like an obsessed gardener wants to protect his priceless gems in their bloom, so a man should want to protect and care for his wife. In doing so she will respond to his care like the rose responds to the gardener. She will bloom just like the rose does.

With this knowledge, who would ever want to strip the petals off of a rose and admire the bare bud naked of its beautiful covering? Also, who would consider presenting such a stripped disgrace as a gift to another? No one would except for an unscrupulous villain. They are the kind who worm their way into homes and gain control over weak-willed women. (2 Tim. 3:6)

The rose, as it is growing in a garden, is most beautiful when love, care, respect and consideration have been included with water, good soil and sunshine, the basic needs of it's life. The woman, like the rose, needs and deserves the same care.

Consider the fool who grasps a rose too tightly and finds his hand (heart) bleeding from the tiny wounds made by her thorns. All the things that the Great Spirit has made are good and serve His purpose, even thorns. A wise man treats a rose (a woman) gently and with care as if she were a piece of fragile blown glasswork set out for display. She can take the bumps and bounces of life and is strong and tough enough to handle any situation but she likes and must have the respect and the honor of being treated as a weaker partner. (1Peter 3:7) The Great Spirit made the woman to be like a rose with thorns for a good reason. In a figurative sense, she can use them to gently prick us men into shape. The Great Spirit programmed her to be the one to set the standard for our acceptable behavior. She can lovingly but pointedly stand as the Great Spirit measure for ethical and moral character. Whatever a woman accepts is the way that a man, mankind, is. Generally speaking of men, we would all be heathens if it weren't for the mother, girlfriend or wife in our lives. Again, I think that her ability is definitely a Great Spirit given gift. That gift, however given, is not indelible. It can be lost as the result of her own wrong behavior, which is often caused by being abused and mistreated by men. A woman who follows the Great Spirit's general moral principles will not accept less for herself than that which is acceptable to Him. These principles are often defined by various religions by different but similar descriptions. Paraphrased and abbreviated one observes moral principles to be "honesty", "commitment", "responsibility" "faithfulness", "fidelity" and "integrity". Because woman is the bearer of children she is of primary concern as the Great Spirit's method of bringing all of us into life. He has placed within her an innate ability to detect healthy situations from those that are unhealthy. This ability is not recognized in just human females but is observed in most female species throughout the animal kingdom.

Doing wrong is like tar, you can't commit it or participate in it without getting some of it on you. Any part of bucking the truth of life, whether by her own doing or by a situation where she is the object of some other person's bad behavior, "effect", will destroy her natural beauty and also her Great Spirit's given ability. Wrong behavior will also destroy any man's character and his ability to be the way the Great Spirit's wants him to be. The characteristics and abilities of men and women will be explored and discussed to a further extent later in this book. I want to convey to you how great it is and how necessary it is to begin to understand the way the Great Spirit wants men and women to be. Beginning to understand allows us to respect and have value for the differences in each other. I like knowing that each gender, male and female, is a personal gift from the Great Spirit to each other.

The Great Spirit loves us and wants us to be the way he designed us to be. We all need to realize the truths inbred in our being created and then, circumstantially, we need fixing and restoration because of our dysfunction, the result of not accepting or not knowing the way that we were designed to be.

Through many avenues, the Great Spirit can and does heal many of our physical aliments. Every faith, religious and nonreligious, has many testimonials of miraculous healing. What is more important than physical healing is healing of our spirit or psyche. I call it "mind health". Or better defined as the ability to think correctly. It is amazing that a number of people that have high I.Q. don't have the ability to self motivate or self discipline.

There are many proponents for the theory that life continues after death, whether physical or on a spiritual plane. I am not against or for any of these. I would rather focus on how important life is, here and now. Why waste any of it, precious as it is, on being messed up with regard to our perspective about our selves and those we claim to love. It is apparent from the number of success stories of persons overcoming insurmountable difficulties, physical and mental handicaps, that the Great Spirit must be committed to helping those that have the desire and seek the knowledge needed to overcome. It is often said of an alcoholic that he remains one until the day that he admits that he is one. On the day he accepts and admits he is an alcoholic he begins a mind process that allows him to change the behavior that he has recognized as detrimental to himself. The major step in any of the twelve step programs in use is to admit the problem and look to a higher power. A power beyond oneself is needed and called on to over come an addiction. It is my opinion that this higher power is omnipresent, just waiting for a person to face the truth of their problem and then ask for help. I don't see any other way to account for the disparities in religion and still admit to the uniformity of many changed lives both in and without their numbers.

As the Master Potter, the Great Spirit certainly is not limited to or by religion. Instead, He appears to be more concerned with the molding and fashioning of individual lives than He is with the outcome of religious differences. Instead of worrying about salvation in some future after life we should be concerned about the quality of our life in our present state. It is definitely wrong to base ones mindset for practicing moral character upon the hope of a future salvation.

Moral Character should be practiced because of knowing the "cause and effect" of what it is.

4. THE BEGINNING

According to Genesis, in the beginning, the Great Spirit created man in his own image. From the dust of the earth he formed the man and breathed life into him. In a figurative sense, because he was formed from the dust of the earth he is like a brick, which is also made from clay, the dust of the earth. The clay [dust] man awoke and wondered at all that he saw. He asked his Great Spirit, "What is your purpose for me"? The Great Spirit answered, "You shall be a caretaker, protector and a provider". "What shall I protect, provide and care for asked the man"? The Great Spirit replied, "You see all the animals that I have created, they are for you. You shall name them as you see fit and your dominion shall be over them". The task was easy for the man because the Great Spirit had made him strong and capable, like a brick. The Great Spirit doesn't ask us to do anything except that He has prepared a way in advance for us to accomplish all that He asks. Prior to asking Adam to be a caretaker, protector and provider, the Great Spirit made him with the characteristics that would enable him to do the job. Characteristics such as; "responsibility', "dependability", "physical strength", "determination", "commitment" and "desire to protect" associated with the male mindset of ownership. Men start out at an early age with the concept of "mine". "Mine" what? "Mine", to take care of, to protect, to provide for and to be proud of. Many of these male characteristics are similar to those characteristics that can be associated with the characteristics of bricks. The Great Spirit designed and made man to be solid and committed so that even during hard times he could continue to care for himself and all that the Great Spirit had given him. The Great Spirit saw that all that He has done was good, except it was not good for the man to be alone. He put the man into a deep sleep and from the first man He supposedly took out a rib and made it into a woman. The man awoke and upon seeing the woman he said "bone of my bones and flesh of my flesh". It is likely that he had an unexplained yearning for woman because of the new emptiness he felt inside himself. The emptiness was a result of having lost a rib. At this point, as he looked at the woman, I'm sure that what he beheld would more than satisfy the emptiness that he felt. He looked at the woman and said, "Wow; aha"! "I shall call you Eve because of your beauty, you are the mother of all living". (The name Eve is thought to mean *living*.) Because the Great Spirit had made Adam a caretaker and protector, he now would want to protect and care for Eve. Much different than men today with their minds clouded up with thoughts of sports, stock market, sporty cars and pending bills. Adam was concerned with taking care of and meeting the needs of his new partner. He respected her and realized his need for her. Her desire was toward him because out from him she had come. (Gen. 3:16)

Does a man take care of his own needs, comb his hair, dress himself and feed his stomach? Even so much more should he see to the needs of his wife who is part of his own body, even his own flesh. What man in his right mind says to his leg, "I have no need for you" and cuts it off, then tries to walk. Just as his leg is part of his body, so his wife is part of his body and he needs all of those parts to be able to function as a whole.

For the purpose of understanding, I want to use a little more back ground. The Great Spirit himself designed the committed union between man and woman. Some people, much after the fact, call it marriage, never the less, committed union is the natural result of sexual intimacy between a man and a woman. He made the woman and presented her to Adam. He calls the two, when they have come together in union, "one flesh". There is no other way to obey His command to multiply and fill the earth. In Malachi 2:13-16 it says that the Great Spirit hates divorce, literally meaning a separation of the man and woman who have come together. There is an obvious purpose in the Great Spirit design. That purpose is to create offspring and at the same time provide the protection that the vulnerable infant and the nursing mother require. Therefore it is of no surprise to find out that He hates a separation of the very union that He made as a necessary condition for producing offspring. Even though many people seem to think single parenting is okay, I don't think that you could convince the designer that it is. At best, the situation would be limping by, much less than what would be the optimum. Religions claim that He will not hear your prayers or accept your offerings if you have broken your union [marriage] covenant. Verse 15 of Malachi is of particular importance. I quote "Has not the Lord made them one"? "In flesh and spirit they are His". Why did He make them "one"? It's because He wants godly offspring. It doesn't say that they will have godly offspring, offspring different from what they have, but it implies that they are godly offspring when the two are together as one. This is profound. It is the purpose and the result of the union between man and woman. If you divorce or separate then you are literally destroying yourself in regard to how you are seen by the Great Spirit. This destruction is vivid especially when we accept and understand His creation of the complete man. Paul says that if you are married do not divorce. 1 Corinthians.7:10 "To the married I give this command, not I but the Lord: A wife must not separate from her husband. But if she does, she must remain unmarried or else be reconciled to her husband and a husband must not divorce his wife". He counsels younger widows to marry in Timothy.5: 11,12. The book of Proverbs 18:22 says "He who finds a wife finds what is good and receives favor from the Lord". Marriage is a new beginning for all of us. We make adjustments and changes to our lives that we wouldn't be making if we remained unmarried. The changes and adjustments are part of the interlocking and meshing required to bind us together and make us the one flesh that Genesis talks about. Place your two hands together, fingers up and palm to palm. Then ask some one to pull them apart. Even though you are strong, your hands can be, with a little effort pulled apart. Now place your hands together, palm to palm spreading your fingers and interlocking them with the fingers from the other hand. Tell the same person to try and pull them apart. This is much more difficult and depending on your strength and that of the person trying to pull your hands apart, they may not be able to do it. The Great Spirit intended there to be an intermeshing and changing of our lives, man and woman together. The result being the strength that will hold us together when the struggles of life try to tug and pull us apart.

5. THE BRICK

The example of a brick in this book could be any male person, but for the sake of convenience I'll tell you about myself because I know the story. I was born right after World war II had come to an end, 1948 to be exact. My parents had seen the great depression and money was again tight right after the war. Both of my parents came from families that were hard working and relatively poor. Parents, in their day, were very strict. They had to be, you couldn't be goofing off, every ones help was needed. Discipline was part of survival. There wasn't much love shown in either of their families. During those hard years any exhibition of love was viewed by other's with the concern that maybe you weren't pulling your weight. You weren't working as hard as you should. My father was the first boy after six girls so his dad wanted to make sure he was a man. He expected a lot from him. This over emphasis on masculinity cultivated a macho, tough guy mentality in my father. He felt that he needed to continually prove himself to his dad. The expectations for my father were transferred down to me after I was born. I was expected to be tough, no sissy stuff. Boxing gloves were put on my self and my younger brothers as soon as our hands were big enough that they wouldn't fall off. My dad would try to entice any neighboring kid to box with us. We boys were entered in little buckaroo rodeos where you were plopped on the back of a steer and let go to see how quick you would hit the ground. When you did, no matter how bad it hurt, you'd better not cry. I remember being entered into a horse show when I was about six. After the show was over, because I knew I was expected to win I cried about not wining. I was given a beating to give me something to cry for.

I had an older sister who was injured and died at age four. At the time I was about three. We were just a little over a year and a half apart. I never realized or even thought about it and it is a different issue, but not until recently did I become acutely aware of how much I loved and missed her. At the age that I was I didn't understand how and why she died. It seemed and felt like she just left and deserted me. This began the first step in a fear of rejection syndrome that has continually plagued my life.

To properly understand where I'm going with this story you have to think of me as a little brick. You know, I'm a little square thing with feet and arms. I guess that's why they call us little guys, chips off the old block. My point is that I started out just like the Great Spirit designed and made me to be, a little brick, solid, heavy and hard to move. I usually went around tipping over things and running in to them as if I thought I could bulldoze them over with reckless abandon.

Not obvious to anyone, including myself, my sister's death was one of the first signs of a little crack in this baby brick. During the turmoil of her death my mother could not cope with life. She couldn't get and didn't want any consolation from my father. He was too macho to show her any kindness and love.

Doing so would surely be a sign of being a sissy and he couldn't let that happen. I'm sure that he grieved but he had to keep it inside. He drank. Because of his inability, my mother had no one she could turn to for consolation that should have come from him. My father did not like me. I guess I must have been a subconscious/conscious threat to him. Some fire was added to the whole situation because I knew my mother liked me better than him. This sad story occurs in many scenarios today, where, because of dysfunctional men, mothers carry on an emotional relationship with a male child that should be reserved only for their husbands. At this point I'm not talking about sex. I am talking about a bonding, male-female relationship. In case you are still blind to what I'm saying, it is when the woman confides in the male and the male person comforts and consoles her that emotional bonding takes place. It's the very basics of a man-woman relationship and a necessary element for any continuing male-female relationship.

When we are wrong and we can't admit it, we are prone to do a lot of blame shifting. We can't blame ourselves, that would cause us to have to change, so we have to point out in an effort to keep the spot light off of our own faults. My dad would always point at me insinuating that I was always wrong. Doing so would give him an excuse to beat me. Something that he seemed to relish doing. When my younger brothers and sisters got into trouble then, a lot of times, I would get the beating. Subconsciously, in my dad's mind, I'm sure that I appeared to be his formidable competition. Beating me and getting into fist fights clear up until he was near forty five years in age was a sick fix for his insecurities. During the times I would get beat, if my mother was around, she would try to jump in and save me. Then, as if he had no other choice, he would get after her. The end result, as wrong and bad as it was, didn't seem to bother me too much, because, aside from the pain of getting beat and seeing my mother getting roughed up, I liked the psychological results. After the beatings my mother would pour more affection toward me and would withdraw further from him. In the end, anyway you want to look at it, he would end up the odd man out. Just in case you haven't clicked on it, in these situations there was nothing positive. Everything was negative for everyone.

I want you to know that the conclusions and observations that I'm presenting to you, at the time they occurred, were not acknowledged by myself. The traumatic nature of the events that happened caused me to somehow block most of them out. I wouldn't have ever known or acknowledged anything about them if it were not for the fact that at some point I realized how messed up I was and at that time, I breathed a continual silent prayer for help. It appears to me that would be the reason that the Great Spirit began to do some identifying and correcting in this area of my life.

When you want to get rid of a weed you have to pull it up by the roots. Anything short of getting the roots out will result in the same weed popping up again. In His wisdom, the Great Spirit would want to get rid of all the weeds, with their roots, in my life. The root problems would be the beginning of the events that effectually made me who I was. I hate weed digging. Some weeds are so stubborn, you pull and dig and pull and dig and usually end up falling on your behind. It is embarrassing, hurts and makes you say, "Ouch", but when the area is all cleaned up you feel much better.

Lifeline therapy is an avenue to open the doors of your memory that you have closed. Initially I did not understand the process. It was only after I learned exactly what it was and how it works that I decided to try it. Once you have the knowledge of your negative behavior and have admitted that you have the problems then following the emotional feeling can help you get to the root of the problems. As simple as I can put it, it's a state of relaxation where your conscious mind is able to see what is stored in the subconscious. The experience amazes me. Your subconscious has a video of every event in your life. The video is not blurry or blemished, no matter how old it is. I told the person helping me that I wanted to go back in my mind to the time when I was little and find out why I always feel like I'm lost or abandoned. I was asked to recline in a comfortable chair by the person helping me. I closed my eyes and relaxed. At that point I felt very relaxed but conscious of all of what was happening. I followed the emotional feeling of being lost and abandoned. I could see my self at about 2 years of age outside on the west side of our house. I could see I had on a white t shirt and white underwear. I was asked, who is there with you? I said "nobody, I'm here by myself". Don't you see anybody? "no". Where is your mom? "I don't know". "My dad is coming from the driveway, He's dressed in black, a dark suit and he's drunk". How do you know? "Because, he's tipsy". Then I asked him, "Where's Marsha"? "Shut up"! he said as he backhanded me. Where are you now? "I'm laying down". Where's your dad now? "I don't know, I think he's in the house". What are you doing now? "I'm laying down". Why? "Because you don't get up when he knocks you down". "If you do then he knocks you down again". Why are you outside? "I don't know, I'm hiding". How long have you been outside? "I don't know". Where's Marsha? "She's sick". What's the matter? "She doesn't feel good".

I realized that I felt abandoned by my mother and by my sister who had died at the hospital. At that age I was already so traumatized by my father that I knew that you don't get up.

I am aware of the biblical reference about the sins of the parents carrying on to the third and fourth generation. I have to admit that the concept is true, not because the bible says so, but because "cause and effect" makes it that way. Not blame shifting but addressing reality, the principle of "cause and effect" had made me one messed up, cracked and broken brick.

About three o'clock one morning I was awakened by what seemed to be a dream, except that it was real, I wasn't dreaming. I was seeing things that I had blocked out of my memory. It was like I had gone through a time machine and all of a sudden, there it all was. Of course I denied it all, another effort to block it out, and then the Great Spirit spent the next month telepathically, and otherwise, convincing me that what I'd seen was the truth. When I turned on the radio, there was talk about identical situations, and as I picked up the newspaper, there would be something there. If I had a conversation with someone, the same issues would come up. When I tried to run, the facts would jump out in front of me. There was no way to escape as I had previously been able to do. Finally I sat down, was still and received the message. By now, you might have guessed it, as a child, I had been molested. At the time it happened I didn't understand, I was just a little guy. It also appeared, through the series of events taking place in my life. In my mind I had subconsciously conceived the thought, in a sense, that my mother was my wife. This idea came to an abrupt halt with a result that was long reaching. I would do things with my mother such as touch her the way that married people do when they are goofing around and aren't in front of others. I was always hanging on her in a way that made her painfully aware that my actions could blow the whistle on her. It got so obvious that I'm sure she decided she had better stop. When she did, it was cold turkey with no explanation to me. I could not comprehend why, but the tables had turned against me and I became the odd man out. Talk about rejection. I wasn't doing anything different than what I had done before. I was only doing what she had encouraged me to do. I didn't know what I'd done wrong. All of a sudden I was termed the bad boy. This tiny brick was crushed.

Even the innocent wrong doer is ravaged by the results of bad behavior. My father hated me and consciously he didn't know why. When I was twenty five years old I got up the courage to ask him why he had always hated me. He said, "I don't know, it just seemed that you were always against me". To him I must have surfaced feelings similar to those caused by an old boyfriend hanging around that he could never get rid of. For years my mother continued to reject me because my very presence would remind and convict her of the things she had done with me. Human psychological self-manipulation of the mind allows us to block out troubling events that we feel should never have occurred. To have a part of the troublesome event that you are trying to block out continually in your face is very disturbing and must be dealt with either by ignoring it or by rejecting it.

As I grew older I became the type of person who would do just about anything to be accepted and liked. To be rejected was more than I could handle. I was insecure in dating and in beginning relationships with girls because I took everything too serious. I was fearful, afraid of being rejected. My fear insured that I would get dumped. "The principle, "Cause and effect", destroyed my confidence. If I felt someone was going to reject me and I always did, I was gone before they had the chance. I couldn't stand the associated pain that I would begin to feel. I want to clarify this, the truth is that I really wasn't rejected by any person. My mind would superficially tell me that I was.

Strange how we can bring the past into the present and transfer cloned trauma from it. You feel trauma that really isn't there. Operating with fear of rejection, rather than work things out with a girl, I would just go find someone else. It was like there was a negative spiritual force propelling me. One that I later named, "The head turner". Even when I was involved with a woman, my head would always be turning to see who else would notice me and possibly love me. This was always a catch twenty two because I could never love anyone in return, it was far too risky. For this reason, infidelity in my first marriage became a problem. I had good intentions. I wanted to do what was right but I was captive to my past. It was as if I was hell bent to self destruct.

My wife didn't do anything to deserve my actions, she didn't even have a thought toward rejecting me. I had already rejected myself in her behalf. Just in case you're wondering, this, and similar behaviors, are prevalent in many men and when not dealt with, in any female - male relationship, spell trouble with a capital "T".

The same blame shifting my father had done became part of my lifestyle. I lived in denial. Being a liar to myself and to others was part of the package.

I've been married four times. The first two marriages were plagued with my bad behavior. It plagued me just like an addiction. Lies, blame shifting and defensiveness were bad habits that, as much as I disliked it, then I could not get rid of them.

Being wrong and not being able to admit it takes a lot of defense mechanisms, while being right requires no defense at all.

My third marriage would have been plagued with the same problems as the first two except that spiritual help came to my rescue. It's my reluctant recognizing of truth that saved me from my past behavior and the associated dysfunction and broke the chains that kept me bound to it. Changes began to take place that made a change in my perspective, which naturally effected my decisions and actions. Changes were auto-initiated because of the changes that occur when one is confronted with the truth about oneself. When you accept it then you are changed by it. You are changed as much as knowing yourself allows. One portion of truth was realized when I saw that I was void of natural affection and that I was concerned only for myself[13]. It had never occurred to me before but now I recognized my inability to use terms of endearment in speaking to my wife. These terms are common with people who love each other and are close together. I could not say the words "honey", "sweetheart" or "dear". Even if I thought them, they wouldn't come out. Only corny kid names that I would make up, like, "mookie", who knows what it meant. A real cute name

---

[13] **2 Tim 3:1-3**, You may be quite sure that in the last days there will be some difficult times. People wil be self-centered and avaricious, boastful, arrogant, and rude, disobedient to their parents, ungrateful, irreligious, heartless and intractable; they will be treacherous and reckless and demented by pride, preferring their own pleasure...

that my first wife really enjoyed was "lizard". She was just ecstatic about it. One can analyze and see that a portion of my thinking process and my emotions had never matured past the preadolescent age.

I could not love. I only feigned love. To love was something I wanted desperately to do, but I was unable due to my fear of being rejected. Because of that fear everyone that I attempted to become close with ended up being used and manipulated by me. Love is the natural result of a male-female relationship wherein respect, admiration and commitment are mutually exchanged. I wanted to have some one love me on those terms but because of my dysfunctional condition, I could not love them in return. On one particular day something, some spirit or telepathic thought, got my attention and communicated to me that I was a liar, a cheat and a manipulator. In return I defensively said, "No I'm not, I'm very careful not to lie". "In fact I'm very proud that I don't lie". I was impressed to read

James 1:22-25[14], a scripture that talks about what I call "the sin of omission". To omit is to leave out. To hear the truth, believe it and then leave out doing something about what you have perceived in this book is wrong. When confronted, omitting the truth is the same as not telling the truth. That is unless you are a politician, which of course, allows you a personal exemption. If we follow this reasoning, omitting is synonymous with lying. From whatever source came to me the convicting thought that I was one who would carefully manipulate others by causing them to believe what I wanted them to believe by the amount of truth that I would either tell or omit. If, in the majority of these situations, I had told the whole complete truth then the person or group that I was talking to would have a totally different picture than the one I was causing them to see. It appeared to me that this behavior is similar to the practice of witchcraft, you know, putting a spell on

---

[14] **James 1:22-24** [NIV], Do not merely listen to the word, and so deceive yourselves. Do what it says. Anyone who listens to the word but does not do what it says is like a man who looks at his face in a mirror and, after looking at himself, goes away and immediately forgets what he looks like.

someone. That was exactly what I was doing with the words I spoke or didn't speak. I was making another person be under the spell of what I had induced to them as my illusion of truth. "I didn't lie", I protested. No, you just didn't tell the truth. Sounds like Bill Clinton and his phrase. "No, I never had sex with that woman".

That's what a "con" does, he cheats others by telling only a portion of the truth. Lie and truth all mixed together for the express purpose of deceit is a "con". I was exposed, convicted and sentenced. Reality sank home. I felt overcome. Then I cried out with tears of remorse. At that point in time I made a life changing choice to either tell the whole truth or remain silent. I'm not perfect at it, but what helps me is having seen and being able to see myself for who I really am. Something that previously, I either chose not, or was never able to do.

Picking out, pursuing and then courting a woman was something else that I couldn't do. I would have to wait until one came after me.

For me, that was a lot safer. The feeling of pending rejection was temporarily held at bay. If I could see that they liked me first then I wasn't as fearful. The bad part about waiting for initial attention from the girl is that doing so is a male and female role reversal where the girl is being the aggressor and the guy is being submissive. Another problem with this situation is that the girl who aggressively pursued me is exhibiting a behavior dysfunction that is as messed up as mine. It's another no-win situation.

I was like Humpty Dumpty who sat on a wall. Humpty Dumpty who had a great fall. All of the King's horses and all the King's men couldn't put Humpty back together again. What can horses do anyway? Men and horses couldn't fix me but recognizing the truth about myself is. Truth, when perceived and accepted, can fix most anything, with or without horses.

Humpty Dumpty sat on a
wall, Humpty Dumpty had
a great fall. All of the
Kings horses and all of
the Kings men couldn't
put Humpty back together
again,

"There are ways to a man that seem right
but the end of his ways are death". [Proverbs
14:12] One of man's ways is we figure out how
to limp along within our disabilities rather
than fix them. If it barely works and we can

still make it by then why fix it? We avoid self-confrontation by telling ourselves that we're OK, we're not dysfunctional. This mind set is a big roadblock right in the way of getting better. Thoughts occasionally pop into our heads that haunt us: "Who me"? "Something wrong with me"? Then we defensively respond: "I don't think so, I get along just fine, its those other people, it's all their fault". I quickly realized that when I think there's nothing wrong with me then that's when I can count on it that there is something wrong with me. In changing I dropped my false self-confident mentality, which was my cover up for insecurity. I humbled myself to the fact that I'm a pathetic human. The only thing that I'm confident of is that I know that there's more wrong with me. I know that all men in their ignorance are pathetic and helpless and that I will always need to seek the truth about myself. I may not always know exactly what is wrong but I know I *will find out because* there is help for anyone who asks.

Scripture says that the Great Spirit is the potter and we are the clay. He says that He will mold and fashion us into something worthy of service to Him, Something worthwhile. Its strange how we change, before I began to understand Him I was afraid of what He might make me do. You know, like becoming super religious, joining a monastery or something along those lines. When I realized that He is not demanding anything in those areas, I wanted to do anything that He would let me. I wanted to be of some kind of service. Much later I realized that He doesn't need our help. Still I thought that I would follow the scripture that referred to men being like clay in the potter's hands. I conceptualized that in order to be used I had to become like clay. Meaning that I had to soften up the areas of my mentality that were, quote; "set in their ways". The ability to see myself for who I really was and the realization that I was messed up gave me determination to want to change. Knowing that I needed to change allowed me to be the moldable clay that I knew was needed for change. I mentally prepared myself to be worked over. Logically, I thought it would be much better for me to soften up than to necessitate having to be softened up. I certainly didn't want to spend any of my time in the stomach of a whale like the biblical Jonah did. The Great Spirit has the ability and methods to change us and yet allow us to make the choices that actually effect the change in us ourselves. By referring to the story of Jonah one can see that Jonah, though he was determined not to go to Ninevah, finally, on his own, made the choice to go, even though his choice was circumstantially motivated.

There are many different circumstances that can cause us to end up different than the way that the Great Spirit intends for us to be. There are so many situations that I couldn't possibly name or identify. It is pretty much guaranteed that every one of us has some kind or other of behavior dysfunction, the result of the errors in our past. It is said that "wrong" roams about like a lion seeking to devour those whom it may. No matter what your life has been like, no matter what you have done or what has been done to you, the Great Spirit wants to take away your hurts and pains and restore you to the way that you would have been if nothing had ever happened. He wants you to be the way that He made you to be. For most of us this means what I call, "hospital time". First, He makes a diagnosis of the problem, then He researches your history and goes back to the beginning of the ailment. Then, He shows you His findings and He recommends a procedure for you to correct the problem. The procedure for change may include changing your diet and your habits. It always includes a personal exercise program. Sometimes an operation is required to remove something that can't be dealt with any other way. I've been on the spiritual operating table before. It's not fun to be kneaded in the direction of healing but when a little of the work is done and He sets you to the side to rest a while, You get mighty happy with the changes that have been made. In a sense you feel indebted to the Great Spirit, as you catch a glimpse of what He's been doing with you up to that point. You want to leap for joy, jump up and down and shout, "Hey"!, "Look at me", "I'm different", "I'm a new man"! I like a saying that I recently heard; "I ain't so bad that I ain't no good and I ain't so good that I ain't no bad, but then He ain't done with me yet either. The reality of what I'm saying to most people is figurative. One has to experience some of it and experience the change in order for the whole picture to become real.

Think of a ball player that keeps making mistakes, he looses confidence in him self. Like wise, mistakes make us lose confidence in ourselves. Biblical scripture tells us that the mistakes of our parents have passed on from generation to generation.[15] We really don't need scripture to tell us, it's sensible logic to see that, mistakes cause "effect" and "cause and effect" effects everyone from siblings to close relatives, to anyone associated and then on and on down the line. I was definitely impacted by the effect of

---

[15] **Ex 20:5,..".**I punish a parent's fault in the children, the grandchildren and the reat-grandchildren"...
Ex 34:7,.".and punishing the parent's fault in the children and in the grandchildren to the third and fourth generation"!

"cause and effect", not only down-line from my parent's mistakes, but from associates and from society as a whole. It was impossible for me to function the way the Great Spirit had intended. I was a broken brick. I was not solid like a brick is supposed to be. I was unable to provide, protect, or to love the way the Great Spirit had designed me to. Severed relationships, deviant behavior and destructive "effect" shaped my life. Then the Great Spirit imparted "truth" took all my broken pieces, gathered me up like pieces of a broken brick, wet me with tears of my outcry and made me into new clay. This clay is now being formed, being pressed into the design mold for man. This mold is better defined as being His intent in design for mankind, male and female. His ways, the intent of design, are substantiated by unchanging truth. Truth that is life and life giving. Cast from this mold, I'm becoming, in a figurative sense, a new person. My old broken and deviant ways have begun to disappear. I have become new by the renewal of my mind with particular regard to how my mind functions in perceiving and then making decisions.

I was excited, but I still felt like dirty laundry. I wanted to be clean, which became an outward expression of my inward commitments. I was willing and wanted to be softened and molded. I was overcome with a spiritual sense that for lack of a better way to describe it, made me feel lighter, like a heavy weight had been removed from my being. I felt a sense of joy and a sense of relief, similar to the feeling of having been unwillingly confined for some period of time and finally set free. My new concepts and commitment seemed to be supernaturally etched into my mind. In a slight way I see this being symbolic of the Ten Commandments having been etched, or burnt into stone. In this case, having been etched into a brick, "me". I would say that the Great Spirit, by avenues knowledgeable only to Himself, is making me into a strong and solid brick with His conceptual truths written into my mind and heart as if written in stone. This once broken and useless brick is being remade, with the added sinew and strength of truth. As a new brick I recognize that I have the

assistance of what I would ascertain to be
inner strength that comes from recognizing and
acting within the parameters of defined truth.
This is the inner strength that I previously
lacked. The lack of which caused me to be
unsuccessful in understanding the differences
between men and women. I find that I am
figuratively, primed, to continue observing
His wisdom, something that I wasn't able to do
when I ignorant of the Great Spirit's ways.

Men, just as bricks, need the support and
help of structure. We need the help and
support of other solid men. Together we are
able to encourage each other when one or
another experiences some difficulty. The
concept of male unity is nothing new in many
ethnic groups. It is largely absent in modern
American culture. In many foreign cultures
men continue to have lasting relationships
between sons, fathers, grandfathers and even
great grandfathers. Wisdom, knowledge and
truth about life, women, children,
responsibility and etc. are passed from one
generation to another. This inter linking,
similar to that of bricks being interlocked

together in order to form a structure, is necessary for a man to be able to remain stable in his male role. I like the old song; "*No man is and Island, no man stands alone, each mans joy is joy to me and each mans grief is my own. We all need one another, so I will defend, each man as my brother, each man as my friend*".

Promise Keepers is the name of a group of men who have promised to be faithful as husbands, fathers and as brothers in their faith. They are praying for each other and offering moral support for each other. They are learning to restore much of what has been lost in our society in the area of involving oneself with others and they hold each person accountable for their fellow men. There is help for us if we seek it, when you get a chance look up "Great Spirit" on the internet. There are places where men seem to be able to find enough glue between themselves and other men to help hold them together and keep them in place as a solid piece. Again, the strength of being like a brick interlocked with other bricks works for one unified purpose.

Even at that, because of man's inherent built in weakness, which, more likely than not, was purposely put there so that no man could be an island, man continually struggles to meet the requirements of being the responsible man, husband, father, protector and provider that he wants to be. Here are a few ideas that I have come up with to help myself in my struggle:

1. Have self control, temperance. Do not be distracted by women or by toys or by temporary satisfactions. Set a goal and make a plan to accomplish it. Be inspired by truth, find that which is good and follow it to a destination.

2. Many men have great intentions but the one who succeeds is the one who seeks the will of the Great Spirit, finds it, takes a bearing, sets a course and follows it.

3. Search your heart, your motives and your secret time. Ask for spiritual help to weed out your faults and ask for the help

needed to plant and nourish what you have chosen as your positive aspirations.

4. Do not manipulate or be manipulated, do not control or give your self to be controlled. Do not let your needs and wants have power over you or allow them to replace the concepts of truth in your life. Be a seeker of truth. Look spiritually for wisdom. Make known your needs and what you can't do. Realize that there is help, both spiritual and from those in your male and female relationships. Don't be afraid. You will be surprised at how relieved you will be when you find out that other people also struggle with some of the same issues as you do. It is for this very reason that the many support groups for different problems are so prevalent and successful. Spiritual help does not come with the waving of a magic wand or as the result of a free gift in the mail. Help usually comes in the form of opportunity, which, you yourself, must chose and then you must put forth the

effort to take advantage of any opportunity.

5. Be aware of the temptations that cause you to fail or be distracted. They are all around you and will sneak up on you and catch you unaware.

6. Be square with yourself and with others. You can't place anything on a round object. It will fall off. Being round is like being a person who just rolls with the flow. Square off and take a stand for your principles. If you don't take a stand for something then you stand for nothing.

7. Remember that every person, male and female, including yourself has buttons. There are fear buttons of various kinds, fear of rejection, fear of abuse, fear of failing, fear of emotional pain and others. There are anger buttons, ego buttons and various dysfunction buttons. Identify your personal buttons and defuse them. Take control over them rather than

letting them control you. Be aware of other people's buttons and discipline yourself not to push them, especially in a desired relationship. Pushing behavior buttons is a good way to destroy any relationship.

8.   Finally, remember that as a human, you must continually review, re-evaluate and redirect yourself. It is amazing how something that at one point was so impacting in your life, can, in a matter of a week or two, be almost forgotten.

These points set the stage for discussing the Great Spirit's design intent for the woman, the female counterpart that a man chooses to become a literal part of him self.

6. THE ROSE

The rose in this story could be any one of you, if you are a female, but rather than tell about just one individual, I want to use a compilation of the women's lives that I have known and have been familiar with.

Young girls are so much different from boys. They are dainty, petite and for some reason they potty train much easier than their male counterparts. I had an older sister and have two younger sisters. Having sisters does not, however, make me an authority on them. Just when a man thinks he has women figured out then they change. Changing their mind and their clothes often is one of their most observable characteristics and is observed in action even at an early age. It appears to me that most of their changing at young age is done with clothes and minds. As a mature adult they are changing again with clothes and minds now that men are included.

When I was pre-adolescent my younger sister would follow me everywhere. She was like a shadow, when I would stop and turn around there she'd be Looking up at me with those big brown eyes. To her I was a hero, in her mind I could do no wrong. I knew better, I could and often did. She was always very gullible and quite game for my many con-jobs. Just about anything that I would ask her, she would do. The knowledge of this fact was food for my scheming mind. It appears that naivety is one of the traits that the Great Spirit designed for women. If it were not for this trait, then, how else would the Great Spirit get them to marry a man? This is funny, but it is not a joke. I'm serious. Naivety has good and bad points. One of the bad points is that naivety makes women susceptible to being taken advantage of. Being male, I was, of course, always guilty of doing that. One of the terrible things that I did to my sister was when we were staying at a motel in Heber City. Our parents sold their farm and got the motel, in part, as trade. Everything was a new adventure so the two of us were scouting around. We found a room that had a lot of paint and fix up things in it. There on a shelf was a partially filled coke bottle. She didn't see me pick it up and smell it to see what was in it. The dark, syrupy fluid looked like coke but it wasn't, it was oil. All my sister saw was that I had a coke and she wanted some. "Please", she begged. "You already had a drink cause I can see it's half gone already". I played along with her gullibility as I sneaked my thumb over the top of the bottle, tilted my head back and held it to my mouth while I feigned taking a big swig. "Uummm", I exclaimed! "Come on, gimme some", she said, with pleading looks and eyes almost in tears. "Ok", "Ok", I said, "But you have to take a big swig like I did, cause I'm only going to give you one turn". I handed her the bottle and desperately tried to keep a sheepish grin from exposing my trick scheme. As I held the bottle out, she grabbed it and without a second glance, took a big drink. At first I felt like bursting with laughter. I couldn't believe that she just did it. She didn't even smell it or anything. Suddenly I realized that she had trusted me. Naive trust that believed that I wouldn't let anything happen to her that would hurt her. Her naive trust made me feel bad as I stood there watching while she gagged, choked, spit and cried. I got scared and began to think that she might die or something. Maybe it was poison oil. Her face was real red and she was stooped over, still trying to spit out the oil. As I reflect back on the situation, the red in her face may very well have been furious anger. Suddenly she straightened upright, took a deep breath of air and boldly spouted out. "I'm telling". Then I was really scared! Nothing is worse than getting a beating from dad. I finally got her to settle down and keep quiet by promising to get her a real coke all of her own.

A woman always looks for someone to trust and then continually tests the water to see if the someone she trusts can still be trusted. Innately, she wants to trust. The Great Spirit designed her to be that way. When you think about it, the need and desire for trust and someone to trust, is magnified when a woman becomes pregnant. Of course pregnancy doesn't make her completely helpless but she will feel safer and a lot more at ease if she has a relationship with someone she can trust. Someone she can count on as a supportive friend. That, in it self, will make her feel safe. I don't think that women consciously think about it but underlying their motives in all they do and say is the root feeling of vulnerability. The vulnerability and the subsequent need to feel safe is why, early on, a woman looks for someone to trust. Older men are often attractive to younger women because they appear to be more trustable. They are accepted and fill the void of a father figure. Subconsciously a woman knows that at some point in her life she will need that trustable person to be there for her.

I pity the women who have been involved with male persons who have shown that they can't be trusted. These men are the ones who have taken advantage of them by playing a game of a solid relationship and then have left them with a child or two while struggling to get by on their own. There seems to be an increasing number of flaky men. For this and similar other reasons, women don't want to have a male person part of their life. Dysfunction in men breeds dysfunction in women. If, perchance, someone does come along that could be trusted, the woman who's been once offended isn't going be apt to buy the next apple. A man, like an apple, may look good and tasty from the outward appearance and she might be tempted but memory of the nasty, rotten apple she last bit into keeps her wary about taking any further bites. Comprehending the facts we have discussed, as they are prevalent in our society, is one reason why I feel that second and third attempts at marriage tend to be difficult and prone to failure. A woman's memory is self-protective. It is often said; "she has the memory of an elephant". The truth is that she may forget many things but she never forgets something that has hurt her or violated her. She never forgets anything that makes her feel un-safe.

Trust has to be part of the marriage foundation. Many women that have been hurt in a previous marriage can't find it within their ability to open back up. When a woman is hurt it goes much deeper than it does with their counter part, men. Men are surface, we hurt easily on that surface but the hurt doesn't go so deep. We can forget and go on. This difference is a specific part of the way that the Great Spirit made things. A man who understands what we have been talking about won't be quite as able to be befuddled with the way a woman acts towards him as other men are when they don't know and understand the nature of a woman.

A friend of mine recently was married to a wonderful woman. Individually they each appear to have a good relationship with each other, which is evidence of a strong commitment to each other. They both had been married previously. I feel that her commitment to him and for the marriage is genuine and that her intention is to trust him and be open with him. Just as we have been discussing, she was looking forward to being able to trust someone. However, shortly after the marriage, for no apparent reason, she rejected him. They are presently struggling to find out what the problem is. He thinks that it's something that he has done, and maybe it is. He could have been insensitive, forgetful or unappreciative. Usually those are simple and forgivable things. More than likely it's something that someone else had done to her in the past and it never surfaced as a problem because no one ever got close and intimate enough to be able to press in the untouched area of this hidden wound. Abruptly the closeness of their new intimacy became just more than she could cope with. All she knows is that "ouch", something hurts and he seems to be the one who is doing it. She is right, something does hurt, but it's probably not his fault. He just happens to be the person in the arena of her vulnerable closeness and by being there as her husband, he, unknowingly, is touching the wound that was left as a result of some particular circumstance from a time before. These types of wounds are often spiritual wounds but they are perceived in a physical or emotional sense. It's very easy for her to transfer, shift the blame of the pain and hurt from the past to her present husband. The blame shifting of the hurt and pain from her past is not perceived by her because she isn't consciously trying to focus on the past. In fact she's trying to forget the past even to the extent of literally blocking it out. It was in this same way that I subconsciously blocked out parts of my own childhood just as if they had never existed. My wounds, however, could not be completely blocked out. Even though the memory was blocked or hidden, the pain never went away.

I didn't think there was anything wrong with me until someone got close enough to me to begin to press in the tender area. In my case they didn't even have to exert much pressure, I would, out of self induced fear, pull my own, "Pain chain".

Anyway, back to my story. The new husband, not perfect but not guilty, gets blamed as the perpetrator of her pre-existing pain that she begins to feel again. She feels present pain that is solely linked to her past. Her reaction is confusing to her, of course she doesn't understand what is happening. All she knows is that she hurts and she feels like she can't stand to have him around. Now then, if he's a strong brick, if he has compassion and has some basic understanding, he will, instead of taking the rejection personal, back off and give her some space. He needs to be committed but not be controlling. If he feels that he loves her too much to be able to stand the rejection then that is evidence that he doesn't love her at all. He's just looking out for his own needs. It is important to realize that caring for someone and, at the same time, trying to have control over them, can not go hand in hand.

She needs to see that, even though he has been rejected, he is solid and unwavering, still able to be her friend. He should show her that he can get out of himself and be there for her, waiting for the time when she is ready to allow him to be close. Being close has to be according to her timing and not his.

The situation can be compared to ourselves as it is for us in our relationship with the Great Spirit. In most situations we are all compelled to wait on His timing. His timing is perfect and right and ours is not.

This man, the new husband, should seek the Great Spirit's help and will and then wait on both Him and her. That phrase in scripture about the first shall be last and the last shall be first and you shall in no way be served unless you first learn to serve all of a sudden becomes clear as we adopt some new perspective.

My first wife had not been married to anyone before we were married, but she had been living with a man. She became pregnant and ended up getting an abortion. This caused another problem to be piled on top of the first problem but more important to this discussion is that another wound is added to the first. After her and I were married we slept together and consummated the marriage but the honeymoon was a disaster. She had all of the best intentions and had no idea that this would happen but after having been intimate together her spontaneous and immediate reaction was that she didn't like me and because of intimacy she felt trapped in what was registering to her as a painful situation. This unmerited response wasn't because of anything that I had done but was because of the painful wound that had occurred as a result of her last close intimacy with a person who violated her and her trust.

At the time I didn't understand and didn't know what was happening. I took the marriage problems personal and failed to look beyond her rejection. Now, as I look back I can see the whole picture very clearly from my great hindsight. The first year of that marriage was terrible for the both of us. When we would go to bed at night she would tell me not to touch her or else she would hate me and never forgive me. I didn't know how to react. I didn't understand women, didn't know myself, was self-centered and was already a broken brick. I also didn't have the Great Spirit's help in trying to deal with what was happening to us. After about a year and a half of steady rejection I felt that the marriage was hopeless and I wanted a divorce. Because I didn't press toward intimacy and, on the front, was kind and considerate, she finally did come around and began to love and trust me. By then I was too hurt with my self-inflicted pain to be able to accept her change of heart. A divorce was the outcome.

Women are communicators. It is one way to comfort concerns and their fears and their way of, at the same time, prodding a prospective male in order to establish his ability to provide her needed trust and safety. Many times a woman wants to communicate to another woman about her problems with men. Generally her desire to talk to another woman is the result of not feeling safe and secure in her environment with the man that she's in a relationship with. For this reason she wants to have another female viewpoint on conceptualizing her own safety. Her unanswered question is: "Am I safe and is this a good relationship for me"? You may not believe it but most female friendships are based on both confiding in each other about the men and children in their lives. A woman wants talk to somebody that she can trust, someone who won't take advantage of the needs that she has. The desire to communicate is a characteristic that is also part of a bonding mechanism that the Great Spirit designed to knit male-female relationships together. In any relationship, if you can talk, you can work out just about any problem. It's when you can't or don't talk that relationships and marriages fall apart. If you are the husband and you won't talk, she will eventually have to talk to someone else. Good advice for women in this situation is to talk to a member of their own gender and not seek a male companion to lend a listening ear. Wisdom, would also be to use any "off time" in relationships as an opportunity to seek a closer relationship with the Great Spirit, rather than, as most do, use it an opportunity to get into trouble.

The work place, where women and men are working together, is often riddled with affairs that seem to have started out innocently as just casual conversation. Both men and women fall into this trap. She needs to talk. He's there and so he listens. She tells him about what a terrible husband she has, what a disgusting thing he did, or how insensitive he is. She can talk about any other number of things that are on her mind and generally does so as long as she feels the listener can be trusted. The listener readily relates to her, he's looking from the outside in and gets only her view. He thinks, "Oh, you poor thing, I'd never be like that". Or, he thinks, "I'd never do that", or "that is just terrible, I can't believe someone could do that to you". It is a necessary part of a man's nature to want to protect a woman so he naturally begins to act protective with her. She begins to think, "he's so nice, he's not at all like Bozo, he'd never do the things that Bozo has done '. Now the trap is set. In case you haven't recognized it, unknowingly, these two people have already begun playing husband and wife roles with each other. The man is being like a husband to her by listening and being protective and she is being like a wife by confiding in and trusting him. Even though they haven't slept together the affair has already started. This blindness on both their parts makes them an easy target for the liaison.

Women are vulnerable, therefore the willingness and gullibility of a girls youth needs to be protected. This is why parents are so important. A good father is of utmost importance in a young woman's life. For him to just be there and be a safe place for her teaches her who she can and can't trust. When there isn't any father a girl doesn't have a chance to learn to trust a man. If the father that is there is not a safe place for the girl she will learn, by the time she's an adolescent, not to trust. Because of these kind of situations the trust she is looking for will always be elusive. Always sought, but never acquired. In some, but not all cases, she will end up being involved in a never ending cycle of relationships that never work out. They will plague her life, like in the old movie; "Looking for Mr. Goodbar".

I have a good friend who has a reoccurring dream. She is on a big ship and everyone is having a big party. The ship begins to sink and while many are drowning she finds herself in a life raft. She turns and sees that there is a man in the raft with her, she's pleased with that and wants him there. She doesn't want to go it alone. As she turns around again to see who he is, he begins to fade away and eventually disappears. She's left all alone. She thinks that this must be the plan for her life, to be alone. She doesn't realize that this dream is an explanation of her relationships with men. She's looking for someone to trust, not overtly, but it's in the back of her mind. Her criteria is high because she's been hurt before by having let go to someone who was less than honorable or by having been let down by an absent father or an abusive brother. Time passes because she's not the dating type. It's far too dangerous. Then she meets someone who appears to be everything she wants. Someone she could possibly trust. As she put it herself, someone she could submit to. She's all excited about him, but after awhile she finds out that he has a few quirks, minor faults at best. He's not perfect so she's not going to be able to allow him into her life. Because of her past hurt and pain her criteria is moved up scale to the state of expecting perfection. This is the form of criteria where she can be assured in herself of not being hurt again. The faults that he has don't have to be real, nor do they have to be his. She can and will superimpose some from somewhere else. She must or else she can't justify getting rid of him. Which is not what she wants but is what she is, by self-preservation, trying to do. If she can make the person out to be bad then she can tell herself that she's good for having removed him from her life. She can, and does pat herself on the back. In this way she keeps defending her critical nature to herself as good. She tells herself that it is her only avenue of self-protection. Which is a self induced misconception. It's a lie because she isn't protecting herself. She's hurting herself by confining and imprisoning herself to a life of loneliness. Right here, Truth, if it could be accepted, would say for her to let go of her fears and attempt to trust him. Even though we're educated and try to be sensible, because of old wounds, we still don't dare to let go. When contemplating letting go we actually feel like were going to die if that self-protecting part of us lets go. That understanding is part of the ticket. It's a key. It has been said that to live you must die, you must die to yourself. That means to let go. Be brave and go right ahead. If you fall, you won't die. It is part of life. Consider the unconditional love that a parent feels and gives to their child. They step out in boldness, without fear of being rejected. Why? Because a parent's well being is not predicated on the acceptance and trust that comes from their offspring. Even if we have to discipline the child, we know that as long as they are young, we are still needed. That assurance allows us to be free from a co-dependant relationship with a child. However, now days, one observes both male and female single parents acting somewhat co-dependant with their children because of the failure of a marriage. This is a situation that a perceptive child soon learns to take advantage of. Once a child learns to take advantage it could carry through from there to their adult relationships.

We have to get back to my boat story, my friend's dream. In truth, the man in her dream doesn't get out of the boat and he doesn't fade away. She fades him away. She refuses to see him any longer. In reality whenever any one does get close to her she feels afraid that she will be hurt. She wants to love but she can't even use the word. It has too much pain attached to it. She can't take the chance. She rejects a man before he can get into any position that causes her to become vulnerable.

Is this a paradox? Yes! Inside she is in turmoil because what she really wants she keeps away from herself. So, she learns to be colder and her heart gets more callous. She can send a verbal piercing dagger, that is intent for her protection, his or anyone else's way without even batting an eye. At one time, in her youth, she had been open, trusting and vulnerable. She was deeply wounded by the person in whom she had placed her trust. In her head there is a mental "mind liar" that comes to help her despair. The mind liar is herself speaking to herself. Subconscious to conscious; "I will see to it that no one can ever hurt you again". "Just build a wall of defense, don't forgive and please don't let any one in". Truth, accepting it and facing it, is the mortal enemy of the "mind liar".

I know a lot about this area of the mind because I have had a similar struggle within myself. A struggle that kept me from being able to love and be loved. In myself I learned to call it "The Pain Chain". Anytime at all and usually for no reason at all, I would feel hurt, a deep excruciating pain. It was not physical pain but a pain in my innermost feelings. The pain would cause me to react in a defensive way as if I was trying to protect myself from some impending disaster. The pain was real to me but surreal because the disasters I feared never existed. I wasn't being rejected and no one had pulled my pain chain. I would, in my subconscious mind, just pull it myself. Thanks for the Great Spirit's mercy. I feel that He caused me to see truth and be able to accept it. It was truth that set me free and truth that required me to "Let go of that thing". I didn't want to but by letting go the chains that bound me to a rut of despair were cut loose. If you allow it, truth can break your chains too. Whether they are the same as mine, hers or different. But you have to be brave, face the facts and quit holding on to what is robbing you of the life that you should have, the life that you deserve. Life that is more fulfilling. Realize that if you get out of yourself, and quit being self-preserving then you can trust in someone. It's not a guarantee that they will never leave you nor forsake you. If that happens you will be strong enough to make it through. The Great Spirit's plan for us, when observed and followed will bless you, heal you and prosper you, not hurt you. You need to understand what that plan is and then let go and be yourself. It's the way that you were made to be.

For a man to regain trust that he has lost or win the trust of one who has been hurt he will have to earn it and keep on earning it. Depending on just how much oil she [remember my story about my sister] drank as a kid will relate directly to how much time consuming and difficult the task of reconstructing that trust will be. Truth doesn't just win us over and then stop. If it's genuine truth, then it keeps on winning us over, keeps on convincing us, even after we have begun to accept it.

Men should be angry at their own gender for the way that some of them act. Such actions reflect on and effect those of us who are innocent of the atrocities belonging to our cohorts. When a woman has been abused it is generally at the hands of a man. Such abuse has a tremendous and lingering effect on how she reacts in the future to other men. The prevalent abuse can be figuratively compared to the breaking of a horse that has been started out wrong. It is much more difficult and sometimes impossible to undo the wrong and get things going right. The word used for such a horse is "soured"! Both men and women can be started out wrong by some of the unfortunate events that have happened to them in the past. This causes their future ability to interact properly to be "soured". Another good word that could be used here is the word "spoiled". Many lives and relationships end up spoiled and ruined by prior things that have happened to us. These are things that we couldn't forgive or forget and can't leave them in the past. Men seem to be able to recuperate from being "soured" a little easier than women. It's probably because men are rather dense anyway. When a woman is hurt the wound goes deep and leaves scars. Women aren't made like bricks. They are roses. Bricks can be bumped around a lot. Roses are easily damaged both physically and emotionally. They're supposed to be weaker and for that reason need to be and should be protected and taken care of. At this point some woman will be upset with me as she tries to assert that she is not weaker. I did not say less than.

Being cuddly and lovable is another trait that I have observed in most of the feminine gender. Boys have been known to do all kinds of horrible things to cats and dogs, but girls find them, bring them home and fix them up. They love to bandage, clean, and feed all stray pets and find it unbearable if one happens to die. It's not that boys are totally insensitive, it's just that girls are so much more sensitive. Sometimes I would be surprised by my sister, who, for no reason at all, would just come up and give me a big hug. I could see and feel that she really loved me. I could see it in her eyes. I've looked into women's eyes and when they love you the look is melting, soft, trusting, esteeming, vulnerable and miles deep. With that deep and vulnerable look she virtually places herself in your hands. It's a look that includes submission, trust, admiration and love. A look that, at times, has struck me deep down and has soberly scared me as I realized all of the implications that were involved.

To submit to a man is the way that the Great Spirit made a woman and the way He wants her to be. Her desire is to her husband. This explains what was meant when the biblical Paul said, "Women, submit to your husbands in everything".(Ephesians. 5:24) He's saying to place your self in their hands, submit to their care, to their provision, to their love, to their commitment. He tells men, "Husbands, love your wives". He relieves women from the responsibility for what happens to them in this open act and places it squarely on the head of the man. When she is submitting, then a man must also submit. He submits to the Great Spirit because He is holding him accountable. We look to Him to meet our needs, to care for and protect us. He will not be in our life unless we submit to Him and his plan for us. In the same way a man cannot be a husband unless his wife places him in that position. I'm convinced that many men are married but they are not husbands because their wives won't put them in that place. It happens when you recognize the position like you recognize a police officer when he is in uniform. That's an idea, men should wear uniforms. A policeman should wear the uniform to represent what is inside him not what is on him. Men, then, should be husbands by what is inside them, characteristics and attributes similar to some characteristics of the Great Spirit. In Webster's New World Dictionary the word husband has interesting definitions: 1. Householder 2. A manager 3. To manage economically, to conserve 4. To cultivate. The definition also includes; *"married man"*.

I can see that the teaching on submission can pose as a threat to some women, particularly any that have, at one time or another, been taken advantage of by thoughtless and selfish men. Women, you can rest assured that "Effect" will deal with all that any man does that is wrong and I sure would not want to be in their shoes while it does. 1st Peter chapter 3 shows how a submissive woman can be used by the Great Spirit to bring about a change for good in the life of her husband. If you read it you will find therein an attitude of submission and of trusting in the Great Spirit.

In a marriage there is a mutual submission to each other, for each not to be abused or be taken advantage of and to be taken care of. For better or worse, in sickness or health. In order for a woman to submit to a man the man must first give up himself. In this illustration, even though the brick is larger and stronger the woman is growing out of him when the brick lays down him self. It's a win-win situation that necessitates that both the brick and the rose give up some of their selves.

The brick lays down his life for his wife

When a woman is treated wrong she can be expected to be angry, hurt and disappointed. If she can't forgive you the warm look in her changes to a hard cold look. Her eyes become impenetrable, like ice that won't melt. Not a good thing and not easily overcome. A scripture says for fathers to not exasperate their children (Ephesians. 6:4). I would suggest that you don't exasperate your wives either.

Of the three women that I had been separately married to, two of them had been sexually abused as children. The same two also had never known their real fathers but had only known stepfathers. One of the stepfathers was an alcoholic. He was irresponsible and abusive. The results of his actions can be seen in her life and is seen in the lives of other women who have been abused. One became a police officer in an effort to right the wrongs of her abused childhood. Her determination and dedication as an officer was a vehement statement of anger and disgust for those who abuse and mistreat. As a child she never had the opportunity to know a man who stood for right, who provided, and who protected. When men aren't the way they are supposed to be they force women to fill the shoes that they leave empty in some other way. Now she would protect herself and others with a uniform and a gun. To win her trust was never possible. Being a man in her life was the most difficult ordeal that I have ever experienced. She required a state of perfection from me that I could never obtain. She presented a false front of quality about herself, while condemning and criticizing others. Expecting them to be as good as she represented that she was. Her heart was like thick cold steel, unbending and unyielding. Sometimes she reminded me of a TV character on the show Happy Days, "the Fonz", he couldn't say the words, "I was wrong". Who is responsible for the way she is? Men are. I shouldn't call them men, they really aren't men as the Great Spirit would have described men. They certainly were not bricks.

I think of one woman that I have known to be open loving and vulnerable and then, without any visible reason, she would retreat into a cold, heartless and indifferent state that is void of any natural affection. How do we become so void and how have we become such lovers of ourselves. We are taking control of our lives with a deviant mindset that has come from the abuses that we have suffered. We place a self-preservation wall in our lives to keep us from ever being hurt again. We don't dare venture outside this wall. In the case that I just mentioned one woman did venture out and had a chance to feel the joy of some genuine companionship but fear caused her to retreat back within her confines. She made a statement that I later understood. She said that what was happening to her was too good to be true. Many of us who have been abused and treated poorly have trouble receiving any good that is intended for us in our life. We don't believe that we won't be hurt. Down deep inside us past pains still dictate our present actions. We are robbed of the things we want by our own negative programs. We are robbed by the very mechanism that promises to protect us. I have mentioned that I believe in the super natural. I believe that there are both positive and negative spirit forces. When Truth combats lies, then negative spirits don't have any further control of our lives. Truth is the positive spiritual force that drives out the negative. Some individuals call this concept "spiritual healing". In some sense I agree because I know that emotional wounds exist. When the negative is exposed and removed then the wound begins to heal. Consciously this amazes me, especially when I know that some spiritual wounds are very old. Only when the sliver is removed can the wound heal.

I picture most of the women that I have known as having once been a beautiful rose, a bud beginning spread it's petals to bloom and then a storm of violence comes too close. Dark and raging the storm came and wreaked havoc with everything. The once tender and beautiful rose is stripped of green leaves and it's petals of soft fragrance. Petals have been torn from around the rose's hip. Arched to one side and nearly broken, she still stands. She has great inner strength. She lives but she can't give anymore. She can't be open and vulnerable. All she had to give has been stormed away. Whoever comes by and sees her knows that she's a rose but they can't delight in her beauty, she's to critically hardened in her heart and if they come too close they will feel the prick of her exposed thorns. She'll stay that way until time brings a new season to her life and the love of a caring, dependable and protecting gardener gently restores her trust and innocence. This gardener is not a man. He is beyond reproach. He is trustworthy and from him comes no harm. He is the Great Spirit and He has a green thumb.

Women tend to categorize men the same as men categorize women. It's unfair but is a trait that we use all too often. Even in writing about men and women I find I have to fight being guilty of the same. This is an effort to describe and understand each other, so if you are reading this, please don't feel that I have put you in a male or female box or that I portrayed to you that the Great Spirit made you all the same. With all the characteristics that define us to be similar in psyche with our own gender we still deviate by having the attributes and personalities that make us each individuals. As such, each of us are unique human beings.

A ROSE IS SAVED

It was not by chance that I came to see
this rose that was created by thee.
She's a rose, but not like she used to be,
she got lost in life's complexity.
Her slender stem is slightly arching.
Her leaves are silently dropping
and her petals are almost gone,
but the life inside her is still hanging on.

She's cried so many tears
and lived a time lost within her fears.
Don't touch her or she'll react,
by piercing you with a thorn still intact.

Then I saw him as he came so near,
he touched her and cried his own wet tear.
He knelt as if, I thought, to pray
but gave her his life on that day.
He latter was taken, they said,
to a grave wherein He was laid.
I'm not sure because I stayed
to watch that rose as she was arrayed
in all of the finest splendor
that is part of her feminine gender.

No longer is she so sad to see,
She's now a crimson rose of beauty.
Her color is like His life that was shed
to make her life so vibrant with red.
I don't understand and I don't know how
but I see him come and tend her then and now.
He's the same one who before had died,
but he's different now. He's glorified.

She's a marvel to watch. I can see her grow
She lights up the garden with a warm soft glow.
She's a rose of beauty, just as if from heaven sent,
the way that the Creator originally meant.
I cried in awe, because I was blessed to see
a miracle that happened right in front of me.   C.F. Hancock

7. IN THE GARDEN

In the garden a beautiful rose grew, the garden was open and was without shelter to protect it. The rose was busy making the garden beautiful. She didn't know there was a terrible storm brewing a few hours away. The storm came and blew mightily. Thunder echoed. Lightning flashed, rain and hail fell from dark clouds. Finally, the storm passed leaving behind all of its' destruction. The rose had barely a petal of beauty left. Her bright green leaves stripped and damaged. Her stem arched slightly to one side. All that was left of her was her rose hip and barren thorns.

That same day a brick wandered into the garden. He was on his way to visit his family. Having just finished his schooling he accepted a new job in the city and was excited to celebrate his good fortune with his family. He had seen roses before and he admired their astounding beauty, beckoning fragrance and the way they grew with their long stem supporting their leaves, buds and petals as they swayed gently with a breeze. He had even heard of rose hip tea. Something pleasant and soothing that comes from their kind. Some day, he thought to himself, he would like to have a rose all his very own, petals, leaves and all. Someone had told him "If you care for a rose properly she will flower and bud for years and years". Caring for a rose requires a little pruning, some cleaning, cultivation, sunshine and pure clean water. With all these thoughts passing through his mind he noticed the rose and wondered what had happened to her. She was barely beautiful at all. Suddenly, feeling compassion for her, he had a wonderful idea. He would care for this rose, cultivating and shading when the sun was too hot. The brick carefully tried removing some of the dead leaves and stems around her. The rose wondered who is this square block of a thing pushing and digging around me. With her thorns she pricked him a time or two just to see if he was safe to be near. The brick yelled "ouch" aloud but then he hushed himself because he didn't want to frighten the rose. He tried speaking to her and he said: "be still, I won't hurt you. I'm trying to help you". She snapped back at him "Help"! Help what? I'm just fine. She was just trying to see if he was sincere with his intentions. She knew that bricks can be very dangerous. Some are known to be harsh and take advantage of a rose's beauty. He seemed sincere enough, but she would test him by pricking him. Then he would have to prove himself. The brick was busy thinking of how he could win her confidence. How could he help her if she wouldn't let him try. He gave up the idea of visiting his family and began to care for the rose. He became more intent on winning her trust and confidence. After all, his intentions were honorable. She began asking him all sorts of questions about himself. She asked about where he had been and where was he going. He answered all of her questions the best he could, but some he was unable to answer because he didn't know the answer. She mused at him, "okay, you can clean up here, but don't get too close or I'll have to defend myself". "I have many thorns you know and they are very sharp". He didn't mind, after all he was a brick and bricks are tough. He didn't even say ouch anymore when she pricked him, he just kept on working. He looked at her. She seemed more beautiful and softer. She seemed to be growing a little less prickly. The brick hadn't noticed until now that he really enjoyed this kind of work, especially now that it seemed there were some results beginning to appear. The first several days that he came around her he didn't get anywhere. She wouldn't let him help her and every time he tried she pricked him with her thorns. Now she pricked him less and she seemed happy. She looked more beautiful each day. He thought to himself, I'm rough and I'm tough but with her I'll be gentle and soft. I'll treat her very special so she won't be afraid and then she'll let me get close enough to take care of her without pricking me with her thorns.

She did let him get closer and they developed a beautiful friendship. He really liked taking care of her. She began to make the garden beautiful. The brick helped her by moving a rock here or there or wherever she decided. She also made him some special creations of her own. The brick fell in love with the rose and the rose fell in love with the brick.

One special day, the anniversary of when he had first stopped by, he planned to ask her if she would allow him to take care of her forever. He promised to be kind and caring and promised to protect her from the winds and storms because he had a strong back. If she said yes, he would even build a shelter, of the best materials, for her. He would build a shelter that would keep them safe forever. The brick told her that she was the only rose he cared for. She grew so beautiful that the whole garden took notice. There was a big celebration and everyone commented on how good it was to have the brick and rose in the garden. He had developed her trust so that she let him brush right up against her and she never pricked at him at all.

One day the brick noticed that she had two new buds growing. The brick was sure happy that all of his hard work had paid off. He took extra special care to see to her needs. She gracefully leant a little to one side as the buds grew in size. The brick supported her with his strength and told her what a fine job she was doing as the buds grew. When the buds opened the brick and the rose rejoiced over the health and beauty of them. When they were older, the brick told them, be careful because roses have thorns and the rose told them watch out because bricks can be rough and harsh and bruise your petals. Protect yourself from storms because they can damage a whole garden. Look for the light and find water, it will make you grow.

8. BEING A BRICK

Being like brick is somewhat similar to being like a computer program. Each are designed to perform a certain task but can't perform the task unless the requirements are understood. It's best to go back to the designer's manual and find out how the program is supposed to work. To be a brick you must find the blueprint to see for what and how you can be used. A basic example of this can be found in the book of Genesis where is written how the Great Spirit created Adam. It is of interest to know that the Great Spirit created Adam out of the dust of the earth, formed him into the man and then breathed life into him. The Great Spirit made a brick out of clay and breathed life into it. It's also interesting to find in the book of Genesis that the Great Spirit created Adam as a caretaker, a husband. That is why his characteristics are like a brick. He has a strong back, hands, arms, and muscles to be able to take care of the tasks in the garden. Adams first task was to protect and look after the garden.

Eve wasn't in his life yet but Adam was still performing one of the functions of a brick, being manager of the garden. The Great Spirit calls man the head of the woman and the family. In this case, Adam was head of the family of animals and plants. He was in charge of the garden and everything in it, which meant he was responsible for the garden. The Great Spirit gave Adam all the animals and then asked him to name them as he pleased. He told Adam that all things were for man's purpose and benefit and that man would rule over the animals of the earth, fish of the sea and fowl of the air. Man would have dominion over them. Having dominion over the animals didn't give Adam the right to tell the animals what to do, it only meant that Adam was responsible for them. He was responsible for seeing to their care. The Great Spirit promised to help him and instruct him in this area.

At this point it is easy for me to understand why the Great Spirit showed me that He made Adam like a brick. Adam was solid and unmoved in his responsibility as a caretaker and protector. Adam did mess it up later when he failed to take a leading position with his wife Eve in the serpent temptation. After this he had to also become a provider. Prior to this the Great Spirit took care of Adam's needs. Adam didn't need to till the ground, he didn't have to plant food and live on the bread he made. The Great Spirit provided everything for Adam within the garden and Adam took care of all the things that the Great Spirit had made him responsible for. They had a good relationship.

Being a solid brick is also being a caretaker. A healthy brick is confident in him self and has a good relationship with his wife and children. He treats them with kindness and consideration. A healthy brick always puts his family before him self. A solid unmarried brick has respect and value for a rose and would never do anything to violate or hurt the Great Spirit's gift to mankind.

A brick should never be moved by circumstance or by fear. His place is to stand still. Abrupt movement can destroy the rest of the building. The Great Spirit calls us to be part of a body, or so to speak, part of a building. We should not be moved by anything going on within the building. A brick has power and strength under control. The Great Spirit is able to use him as he stands still in submission to Him for His purpose and plan. Even in suffering the brick is not moved. He is solid as a stone.

It is great to recognize the way that the Great Spirit created men to be and to put into action the program and feel the joy of performing as a solid unmoved source of strength and support.

I think of putting together a new bicycle. There's a box of parts to build it. Even though we read the instructions something usually goes wrong. We can visually throw the bike together but frustration sets in when the shifting mechanism fails to change the gears and instead drops the chain from the sprockets. After making several attempts to adjust the mechanism and finding that it still fails we resort to reading the instructions. Then we make the proper adjustments and exclaim in awe and excitement, "Hey it works! It works"! The same holds true in our life. If we find the directions and understand the program we find out what adjustments are needed in our lives and find out how to program our self to function as we should. Then we will exclaim, "Hey, it works! It works"!

The key that must be included here is the Great Spirit's value system. Men have, in the past, given years of their earnings for just one good woman. Men have fought to their death to champion the woman they love. The Great Spirit gave Eve to Adam as a priceless and precious gift. She was the only woman in existence at the time. I'm sure Adam's value for her was unapproachable. Today this same value must be restored in our minds. Then we can and will be willing to give up part of ourselves for the needs of others. The Great

Spirit's value for us must become the value we have for each other.

This prose explains many of the characteristics that the Great Spirit engineered man to have:

BRICKS

BRICKS CAN BE ANCHORS FOR OUR TROUBLED HEARTS

BRICKS CAN BE PLATFORMS FOR RESTING

BRICKS CAN BE A WALL OF PROTECTION

BRICKS CAN BE A SOLID SUPPORT ON WHICH TO LEAN

BRICKS CAN BE A SANCTUARY, A PLACE OF PEACE

BRICKS CAN SUPPORT A HEAVY LOAD

BRICKS CAN IMPART WISDOM TO A TOUGH DECISION

BRICKS CAN LOVE WITH A HEART THAT'S SOFT

BRICKS CAN SOAK UP A STREAM OF TEARS

BRICKS CAN LAY DOWN OR THEY CAN STAND UP

BRICKS CAN BE JOINED TOGETHER FOR ADDED STRENGTH

BRICKS CAN STAND ALONE AS A SENTRY

BRICKS CAN BE TREAD ON, SAT ON OR ADMIRED IN AN ARRAY

BRICKS SHOULD NEVER BE BROKEN

9. BROKEN BRICKS

Being broken means that you can't sufficiently complete a task. When someone asks why the toast is burnt you say, "Well, I think that the toaster is broken, it doesn't work right". The Toaster might still work it just doesn't work right. Broken bricks are unable to properly take care of anything and are unable to perform in the way the Great Spirit made them. This can be a program error, which is usually a result of the absence of a suitable role model in their life. A proper father image can teach bricks how to be solid. Without this teaching bricks find themselves in precarious positions and end up falling and being broken. We usually pattern our lives after the lives of the adults in whatever kind of environment we are raised in.

There are ways to lay bricks or to place bricks in a supporting function in life. Behavior mistakes destroy a mans confidence and security in himself and can cause him to compensate by being overbearing and controlling.

Making behavior errors or being the recipient of them breaks down our ability to trust others. Someone who doesn't feel well about them self may try to act tough to hide their lack of confidence. They are trying to convince themselves they are ok. This defensive shell actually prevents the brick from seeing reality and admitting there is a problem.

As bricks, when we fail to be solid, responsible and protective, we cause women to find protection in other places. If she can't trust a man to be the way he's supposed to be, she has no other choice than to step out on her own. She is very capable because the Great Spirit made her a helper. So, instead of helping him she has to help herself. Honestly, they would rather be helping him if only he would act right.

Every woman is looking for a man to be like a brick in her life. Females who had loving fathers often want a man to be like Daddy. When men fail to be bricks it causes women to reject them. The Great Spirit placed in a woman a nucleus that discerns acceptability. What is not acceptable must be rejected. Broken roses, violated women find themselves accepting unacceptable behavior from men and this makes them insecure which again makes them vulnerable to unscrupulous men. It is a vicious circle that keeps generating the same negative behavior. Scripture says these men prey on weak-willed women. Women who don't have their nucleus of acceptability in working order. The broken bricks are stripping off petals and leaves from the Great Spirit's precious gift to mankind, the rose. Don't think that he is not upset and don't think that she isn't either. The thorns that are left will get you and you'll find your hands and heart bleeding.

A broken brick is unable to give value to a rose. Negative society aims to make it unacceptable for men to value women. Bricks have shortened their expectations and are unwilling to pay the price for the rose they want in their life. They choose roses on a lower scale where there is no respect for her. Negative behavior destroys us by continuing to erode our respect and value for each other's gender.

Bricks, when broken, are unable to be a safe place, unable to protect and provide. They are irresponsible and are generally selfish, always looking after their own desires.

Paul wrote about having a thorn in the flesh and he prayed and asked several times to be delivered from it. The spirit told him, "My grace is sufficient". I have heard many expositors of the bible try to describe what the thorn in his flesh was. One description was that he had some kind of skin disease and another was that he had failing eyesight and another was that the thorn in the flesh was some of the people that he had to deal and contend with. Personally, I feel that this thorn in his flesh was the same thorn as is in the flesh of all men. Men always have their hormones present. The Great Spirit designed it that way for His purpose, but the effect on men needs to always be in check. Otherwise we become like the rest of the world, given over to lust and debauchery.

When I evaluate the crimes committed by men the overwhelming majority of these are the result of man's sexual drive. He steals things to try and impress and gain a woman's approval. Of course he doesn't tell her where the stuff came from. He lies to cover up all of the details. He wants her approval and in a perverted way he is trying to be a provider. His motivation is part of the Great Spirit programming but with negative direction. Rape, molestation and even homosexuality are all tied into man's sexual drive, which is definitely a thorn in a man's flesh. These are all deviant variants of the sexual drive that the Great Spirit intended for man's good. In order for that drive to be good it must be placed under disciplined direction. Women, per-say, are not the thorn, not the problem, they are the way that the Great Spirit made them. The fact that He made women sexually attractive to the man is a positive, not a curse. The thorn is not man's hormonal drive either and it's not the fact that a man has testicles. The fact that a woman's appearance is stimulating to the man isn't the problem either. The thorn or problem is man's negative thoughts and behavior. The temptation to think wrong thoughts is always present. When married it's very healthy for a man to be attracted to his wife but not healthy for him to be attracted to anyone else. When you're not married and you see a beautiful woman you have to be careful to not begin wishing that you were married. I think you get my point. Testicles don't have a conscience, so you have to use your head. The distraction can be like a thorn in your flesh. I can imagine Paul, who was devoted to his ministry, being distracted by this same situation and wishing, even praying for the Great Spirit to remove the distraction. There is a struggle in my body between the flesh and the spirit. I can identify a major part of the battle as different forms of sexual temptations. That's why Paul said that we must die to the flesh daily. I remember thinking about this very issue right after I became aware of the whole picture. I was afraid of falling short in this area. We all aren't into pornography. We don't all rape and we all don't murder. We all don't steal but we all have had a lustful thought at one time or another. It's one of the biggest weapons against men and an avenue of destruction against the strongest man. Take David for example, a man after the Creator's own heart, yet his eye was distracted to look upon Bathsheba with lust. Adultery with murder and lies became the result of his distraction. Abraham, the father of Israel, tries to fulfill a promise given to him in his own way. His wife said to take Hagar, her maid and servant and lay with her. I don't think that the Great Spirit mentioned to him that he should do that. He hadn't had any children with Hagar up until that time so we can say that he wasn't following tradition of the time that had him laying with the servants. Apparently he had not taken any other wives prior to this time. The scripture says that both he and Sara were older and she was beyond the years of having children. After Isaac and Ishmael were born Abraham took other wives and had other children. Sounds to me like he got a little carried away with the promise. The child that Hagar bore, Ishmael, was sent away along with his mother. Sara found discord and jealousy between her, Hagar and her son. The thought comes to me that Sara also doesn't like the fact that her and Abraham's mistake walks around her daily. Her nature as a woman is to want things to be right. She will move the furniture, shake the rugs and the whole house until things are right. She can't have a clean house as long as Hagar and Ishmael are in it.

Samson, the strong man was brought down by a thorn in his flesh. Don't let anyone try to tell you that it wasn't there. In some cultures men are made eunuchs so that they may serve without being distracted. Male livestock are castrated so that they are more docile to handle. Paul, I feel, was saying deliver me from this thorn so that I may serve without distraction. He says that he would that others could be like unto him self, totally given and dedicated to service. When a man is married he seeks to please his wife and her to please him. He who is not married seeks to please himself. We find no place where it mentions that Paul was a eunuch. He also says that if desire burns within you it is better to marry. Paul's desire to serve, if he were not a eunuch, had to be hampered somewhat by his normal hormonal activity. To some men, that hormonal activity is a thorn in the flesh.

When I thought about these very issues I recognized them as some of men's weak areas. To put this issue in perspective I realize that my eyesight gets weaker with age, my joints and bones ache and my skin dries up and wrinkles. My wounds I bear as medals of my manhood but none of these do I consider to be thorns in my flesh. No matter what age I am a scantily clad woman provokes some tempting thoughts that I have to deal with. The Great Spirit knew what he was doing when he put sex drive there in the first place. It is for the motivation and the drive to be a protector. It is also for species propagation. It is the motivation that a man must have enable him to take care of his wife and family. A stallion gathers and protects his mares, a gelding doesn't. The gelding is docile and quiet. A bull fights with other bulls to rule a herd, while a steer doesn't even care. Being in control of our flesh is a source of strength to go tackle and conquer life's obstacles. Just put the temptations aside and in all instances turn them into positives. Negatives can destroy our lives and cause us bricks to fall into pieces. We can't do our job as men unless we are solid and are placed firmly on a foundation of positive precepts and principles. The Great Spirit wants us to be able to be used for good. He wants to be able to put some weight on us and have us bear up like a brick.

Some interesting facts about bricks are that when they are laid standing up they are called soldiers.

The front of a brick is called the face. Bricks are commonly placed lying down and are run (laid) in a straight and level line called a course.

Bricks have holes in them, usually three, which helps them to bond to each other and to the mortar as they are laid. These facts about bricks also happen to describe similar characteristics in men.

10. BEING A ROSE

The rose is a gift to man from the Great Spirit. In the book of Genesis it says that the Great Spirit saw that Adam needed help. He said "I find that everything I've done is good but it is not good for man to be alone". Maybe Adam was struggling in the garden, or maybe the Great Spirit just had the insight to know. He told Adam "I'm going to make a helpmate for you". When the Great Spirit told Adam this he was excited about the prospect of having a helper and he said to the Great Spirit; "what will this helpmate do"? The Great Spirit answered him saying "she will be beautiful and you will love her. She will care about you, feed you, take care of you and see to all your needs. She will always be there for you and will help you with everything you do. Adam said; "wow, that's a lot"! "What is this going to cost me"? The Great Spirit replied, "Just an arm and a leg". Adam thought for a moment and said; "Oh, that's too much, what can I get for a rib"? Shortly afterwards Adam was walking in the garden, and the Great Spirit came along and said to him, "How is it going Adam"? Adam answered, "Oh great, really great"! The Great Spirit asked, "What is so great Adam"? Adam said; "oh, Eve is, she is so amazing that I just can't take my eyes off her". "Why did you make her so beautiful anyway"? The Great Spirit said, "I made her so beautiful so that you would love her". Adam then said "I really do love her, but why did you make her so warm and soft"? The Great Spirit said again, "Because I want you to love her". "I want you to be so in love with her that you become totally committed to her". Adam said, "I'm so in love with her that I could never do anything to hurt her". Then Adam asked the Great Spirit, "answer me just one more question". "Why did you make her so naive and gullible"? The Great Spirit replied "because Adam, I also want her to love you".

The rose is a beautiful gift. She was not made from the dust of the earth, but was taken from the side of Adam. The Great Spirit made her beautiful. In fact there are not many men on earth who do not take notice. The main characteristic of a rose is to be a helper. She was designed and made to be a helpmate, meaning suitable helper. The Great Spirit made men and women differently. You can look at the physically differing characteristics and get a real good idea of what He had in mind when He made them. A woman has breasts and a uterus. A man has neither. A man couldn't bear a child if he had to. He can help raise them and take care of them but he can't give birth. The Great Spirit designed her with not only the physical equipment to have children but also the mentality that goes with it. The man has a strong back, larger arms and legs. His frame is stronger and is made to be able to stand the rigors of hard physical labor. The Great Spirit made the rose a responder and the brick an initiator. A healthy rose responds to good initiation. A rose has the ability and knowledge to say no to improper initiation. It is not difficult when she understands the way the Great Spirit made her.

Another characteristic of the rose is the great insight she has to perceive all that is going on in the home. She beautifies her surroundings and has a given drive to have everything put into order. This is the Great Spirit plan. Order is necessary so that when a child is brought into the world it will have a safe secure environment in which life can begin. The protection of her womb extends beyond her physical body. The rose is able to perceive things from every direction. She can tune into many areas and tasks at once. Men are tuned into only one thing at a time. Like in a ship where there are many compartments, the woman will know what is happening in each compartment. Men, on the other hand, only know what is happening in the compartment they are in. They can leave that compartment and go to another and know again what is going on in that specific compartment. Men are already forgetting about the compartment they were previously in. This is one reason why a woman is a great help to a man. She has the insight to let him know what is going on in the whole ship, in the family and the neighborhood. More likely than not she even has the insight to tell him what's going on with him!

Men can help raise children but the wife and mother is best suited to the task of nurturing. Men are too dense to perceive the needs and afflictions of little ones. For instance; men don't recognize the diaper is dirty until it is leaking all over. They don't recognize that there is a little diaper rash or that the child is hungry. Men will bounce the child on their knee in order to stop them from crying when the child really has diaper rash or is hungry. The Great Spirit gave the woman all the instincts and intellect she needs for the job of raising a family.

Another characteristic of the rose is she is a homemaker. She makes and beautifies the nest. One woman, a noted speaker who had come from a wealthy background never had done any cooking or homemaking but upon receiving knowledge and belief in the Great Spirit she immediately called her book dealer and ordered two books, a bible and a cook book. She felt a profound desire to cook. Who can say that the Great Spirit did not give a woman or this woman that desire. A woman, at times, will just want to bake a cake or some cookies. Most men don't ever want to make cookies but they always want to eat some. Of the women I have personally known all have at one time or another wanted to bake or cook. In our society we haven't given positive recognition for the characteristics that the Great Spirit placed in the woman. Instead we have made her feel that she should get a career and then she will merit our esteem.

She makes the house a home and puts it in order by decorating the walls, arranging furniture, fixing, creating, sewing, embroidering, painting and using whatever other areas of talent that are within her. Roses all have different talents and they use them to beautify their home and surroundings. The Great Spirit made most all women with the instinct to be clean. Before Eve was tempted by Satan to eat the apple she probably asked him "has it been washed"? I'm sure the snake told her the apple was washed otherwise she wouldn't have taken a bite of it.

Somehow in the makeup of a woman the Great Spirit put in the intuitive nature to establish a safe environment for herself and her children. When a mother cat is ready to have her litter she searches for a safe place. Once the babies are born if this place becomes unsafe she will move the kittens one by one to a place which is more suitable or safe. She is always perceiving and checking for safety. The kittens may be moved more than once and may even be moved back to the original birthing place. A mother hen does a similar routine but adds a lot of picking, prodding, and shifting of the nest before she finally lays an egg. I have noticed that a woman is always checking for safety. Is this man safe? Is this house, this neighborhood, this school, safe? Whether she has a child or not she is continually checking for safety. Like a hen has a beak and a cat has some claws a woman has her nature. The thorns of a rose can prick the surroundings to establish its safety. A woman uses verbal inquisitions to prick at her husband. She may ask the same question many times and get the same answer but will keep asking until she begins to feel comfortable. She may press a touchy situation to remedy it safe. What happens to the man when he is questioned, pressed and prodded? If he is healthy he responds with care and consideration. He helps the woman feel safe by the way he responds. If his behavior is unhealthy he will respond to the questions with indifference, defensiveness and anger. When he does so he is telling her that he is unsafe. His actions cause a bell to go off in her head that says "unsafe" "unsafe". In a woman this whole mechanism of establishing safety is going on subconsciously. She doesn't think about it. It's just part of the way that the Great Spirit made her. When he responds negatively she will continue to question and press him. He may think he's being picked on, but he doesn't understand the way the Great Spirit made her. She has to make things get safe or get the problem out of the nest. An argument erupts and both of them loose even if it's only one or the other that is right. She won't give up either because her motive is not to win arguments. Her motive is to establish safety. Have you ever noticed how some women tend to move the furniture around a lot? If they move it often it is usually a sign of their being unsettled. They are feeling unsafe. Does a particular man complain of his wife's continual nagging? Don't look at her. Her nagging is usually an indication that this man is giving her an unsafe signal with his inability to communicate to her his ability to be and provide safety. Many divorces and separations could be eliminated if men simply learned to respond in a healthy way to the woman's needs. Once a woman has established a secure home around her she will feel comfortable enough to give birth to a child.

Women set the stage for the standard of acceptability. She can say what is and isn't okay. Particularly in setting the stage for bringing life into the world. A healthy rose doesn't want to have children unless there is safety and an acceptability factor in place. The Great Spirit created within her the attributes and the sense to say "I will not have a child in this situation". "Things must be changed". That is why the Great Spirit gave the rose thorns. She can be firm and unmovable and use those thorns to prick at us to make the changes necessary to make her comfortable enough to bring life into the world. The Great Spirit gives the rose this responsibility and makes her able to make the right decisions. There is a Proverb that says that it is better for a man to live on the corner of a roof than to live in a house with a contentious woman. I say that it is better for a man to conform to his wife's standards than for him to have to live on the corner of the roof. If his behavior is unacceptable she will contend with him until he changes or until he moves to the roof. A woman sets the standard for acceptability, behavior, environment, friends and etc. The Great Spirit gave her the drive to establish safety in her environment. What she finds unsafe she will peck, prick and press until it changes or until it's removed. I mentioned that the Great Spirit gave her some thorns as a rose to prick things that are not acceptable to her. I recently became engaged to a wonderful lady. She promptly brought to my attention an item hanging from the mirror in my truck. It was a garter tossed to the crowd at a wedding that I had attended earlier in the year. Both the bride and the groom were friends of mine. When the time came all the eligible men were asked to stand behind the bride. She would stand and throw the garter behind her and whomever caught it would be the next to marry as tradition goes. I stood back behind the others. I wasn't too competitive for the prize. The garter came right at me. In my thoughts I hoped that someone else would catch it, so I didn't catch it. It fell right at my feet. I looked around to see if anyone would dive for it. They all just stared at me with a "It's yours", look. So I picked it up. Later that evening as I left I couldn't help but wonder if there could possibly be something to the old wives tale. I hung the garter on the mirror in my truck and said to myself, "we'll see"! I never much thought about it hanging there, nor did I think anything about the fact that it had belonged to another woman. I was surprised when my fiancee said; "oh, by the way, that garter on your mirror isn't really acceptable for a man who believes in the Great Spirit". She wasn't implying that I was a man that believed in the

Great Spirit. She was saying that if I wanted to be one that believed I should get rid of the garter. I liked what she said. She was right. A engaged man doesn't need to have any other woman's leg-thing hanging from his mirror. It would be in poor taste and disrespectful to his intended bride. During the time that we had dated she never said anything about it. I hadn't thought about it since it was hung there. As soon as we were engaged that made things different and she felt a need to begin to establish safe surroundings. To me this is a characteristic that the Great Spirit has given her, an inborn need to set standards for her spiritual, physical and mental health and safety. Another area that my fiancee touched on was her concern that any of my past relationships could come up and disturb our future. She put it plainly "That woman is not ever going to be calling our house". Without even knowing it she had begun to set a standard of acceptability which included getting rid of the past and protecting the future. She set the standard but then looked to me to perform the function of putting things in order and ensuring protection. I don't think that a woman thinks about it all the time but only she has the capability to bring life into the world. Whether she gives birth or not she will set a standard for surroundings suitable to bring a child into. None of this is a conscious effort on her part, nor is it something that a man does. It's just the way that the Great Spirit made her. Scripture says "Go forth, be fruitful, multiply and replenish the earth". Women are very committed to their tasks. You will find that in the work place they tend to be very efficient. For instance, in the company where she is employed, she will want to help the company succeed. This makes women good employees because they are dedicated to their task and able to complete it. Where men are self-seeking and motivated inwardly a woman is different, she seeks the good of her employer. She is usually loyal, committed and feels good about playing a helping role. At times a woman is torn between her responsibility at work and her responsibility at home. These days we often see the occupation winning out in the battle. The man who wanted his wife to work is now reconsidering his choice when he sees her job become more and more important. He may even become jealous and be at odds with how to deal with the person he thought he knew but now sees changing.

Years ago a woman really had to depend on a man to help meet her needs. Now she finds that she can make it on her own. Many divorces are caused as the result of her finding a career that sufficiently supports all her financial needs. Men, who in the past, have received their ok from providing the financial stability for their family are now intimidated by having to share the turf. The traditional roles for men and women are so changed and modified that it is very difficult to ascertain exactly what they are.

11. THE ROSE OF NOBLE CHARACTER

PROVERBS 31

If you can find a truly good wife, she is worth more than precious gems!

Her husband can trust her, and she will richly satisfy his needs. She will not hinder him, but will help him all her life.

She finds wood and flax and busily spins it.

She buys imported foods, brought by ship from distant ports.

She gets up before dawn to prepare breakfast for her household, and plans the day's work for her servant girls.

She goes out to inspect a field, and buys it; with her own hands she plants a vineyard.

She is energetic, a hard worker, and watches for bargains.

She works far into the night! She sews for the poor, and generously gives to the needy.

She has no fear of winter for her household, for she has made warm clothes for all of them.

She also upholsters with finest tapestry; her own clothing is beautifully made-a purple gown of pure linen.

Her husband is well known, for he sits in the council chamber with the other civic leaders.

She makes belted linen garments to sell to the merchants.

189

She is a woman of strength and dignity, and has no fear of old age.

When she speaks, her words are wise, and kindness is the rule for everything she says.

She watches carefully all that goes on throughout her household, and is never lazy.

Her children stand and bless her; so does her husband.

He praises her with these words: there are many fine women in the world, but you are the best of them all.

Charm can be deceptive and beauty doesn't last, but a woman who fears and reverences the Creator shall be greatly praised. Praise her for the many fine things she does. These good deeds of hers shall bring her honor and recognition from even the leaders of the nations.

This chapter in the book of Proverbs describes the way the Great Spirit made the woman and intended her to be. This particular woman exists entirely for her family and husband and is known throughout the town as a good woman, a rose of good character. We can look at all the things she is: a beautifier, helper, nester and is a person who can physically bring life into the world and sustain and nourish it. Behind the man who succeeds, the child who excels and the nation that rises is a good woman.

With the struggles that we have in our society today there are many marriages that end in divorce. Even in churches the rate of divorce nearly equals that of the rest of society. My third wife left and divorced me and said that the lord told her to. I don't speak for the Great Spirit but I don't think so. In Corinthians Paul says, "Woman, not I but the Lord commands you, do not separate from your husband, but if you do, do not divorce him. Several other scriptures give similar warnings. Malachi 4 says that the Great Spirit hates divorce. In Matthew it says that from the beginning the Great Spirit never intended for people to divorce. Moses only granted divorce because of the hardness of the people's hearts. So, does a hard heart justify a divorce? No. Here is the difficulty, a woman who is acting in the way the Great Spirit made begins trying to establish her surroundings. The man who is the head is supposed to recognize this as good and healthy behavior on her part. He helps her, but if he is not aware of a woman's character and he isn't recognizing the way he should act. He becomes defensive and feels his manhood is being exploited. She feels unsafe because now he is not help but is a threat to their future. She will be fearful and reject him. When he is rejected his ego is damaged and he doesn't feel like a man. Then he tries to save his ego by using a deeper and louder voice. Instead of establishing himself as a man to be trusted and looked up to he, instead, is feared and despised. A "no win" situation. Here's the key. The Great Spirit has to be the one in control, not the man and not the woman. If they both submit to him then the problem can be solved. Divorces are direct results of both men and women trying to be in control. We already know that there are two spiritual forces in control of everything and neither one of them is us. We know what the Great Spirit says for positive and we know what the enemy wants to do for negative. Scripture says we are to submit to all those who are in authority. Why is it we don't listen and submit to the Great Spirit and his ways? After all, isn't he, "The Authority"?

My greatest and best advice to women is 1 Peter 3:1-7; "Wives, in the same way be submissive to your husbands so that, if any of them do not believe the word, they may be won over without words by the behavior of their wives. Then they see the purity and reverence of your lives. Your beauty should not come from outward adornment, such as braided hair and the wearing of gold jewelry and fine clothes. Instead, it should be that of your inner self, the unfading beauty of a gentle spirit which is of great worth in the Great Spirit sight. For this is the way the holy women of the past who put their hope in the Great Spirit used to make themselves beautiful. They were submissive to their own husbands, like Sarah, who obeyed Abraham and called him her master. You are her daughters if you do what is right and do not give way to fear. Husbands, in the same way be considerate as you live with your wives, and treat them with respect as the weaker partner and heirs with you of the gracious gift of life so that nothing will hinder your prayers". Now that is intense wisdom and advice. What man could not be won over when treated with respect. Respect preserves his ego and when admonished with kindness it melts any hard heart. To back up 1 Peter we can go to the story of Abigail in the Old Testament. She was married to a man named Nabal. The name means "fool". Although I don't think she was the one who named him. He was a wealthy and prideful man and had just brought in a bountiful harvest. King David and the boys, about 400, were in the area routing out squatters and they were short on supplies. They heard about Nabal and sent a few men to go and ask for food and clothing. Nabal, the fool, was feasting and celebrating his good fortune and hurled insults at them and sent the men away with nothing, even though he had plenty. The men went back to David and told him and David said; it has been useless, all my watching over this fellow's property in the desert so that nothing of his was missing. He has paid me back evil for good. May the Great Spirit deal with him, be it ever so severely, if by morning I leave alive one male of all who belong to him. Nabal was still drunk from the night before and so Abigail gathered the servants and prepared food and clothing and went out to meet David.

When she saw him she got off her donkey and bowed down before him with her face to the ground. She fell at his feet and said: "My lord, let the blame be on me alone. Please let your servant speak to you; hear what your servant has to say. May my lord pay no attention to that wicked man Nabal. He is just like his name, Fool and folly goes with him. But as for me, your servant, I did not see the men that you had sent. Forgive your servants offense and accept the gifts I have brought for you and your men. Then she praised and gave honor to David and asked that he not shed needless blood. David said to Abigail "Praise be to the Lord, the Great Spirit of Israel, who has sent you to meet me. May you be blessed for you good judgement and for keeping me from bloodshed. Then David accepted her gifts and request and told her to go home in peace. When Abigail got back and went to Nabal he was in the house holding a banquet like that of a king. He was in high spirits and very drunk so she told him nothing until daybreak. In the morning when he was sober, she told him all that had happened and his heart failed him and he became like a stone. About ten days later Nabal died. David heard what had happened and sent word for Abigail to come and be his wife. The story is of a woman who is married to a man who is a fool, but she doesn't divorce him, she doesn't take matters into her own hands, she instead saves the guys neck, she puts the Great Spirit in charge by her actions. She fits right in with 1 Peter 3. Now that the Great Spirit is in charge he deals with the man. He will and can do the same in your own situation. He may call you to carry the load and bear the burden. This life is short, nothing that we are called to bear can ever amount to anything compared to what He has born for us. If you give it to the Great Spirit he can do it, but if you do it you're blocking anything he could do. His way is always better than ours and he says that he asks us to do nothing except that He prepares a way in advance so that we may accomplish whatever it is he asks.

Sometimes life is a burden that we are all called to bear.

12. WILTED ROSES

Wilted and soiled roses are those women that have been mistreated and abused. This happens when negative men initiate and the rose is caught responding to the lies and promises of such unscrupulous men. If she is wrong in the way that she responds she sets herself up for abuse. The Great Spirit wants to teach us all how to say "no" in wrong situations and how to say "yes" in the right situation. In the world today, we find broken initiators, bricks, who are initiating negatives and roses who are responding to it. The Great Spirit wants the bricks to stop initiating wrong and wants the roses to stop responding to negative initiation.

When the rose is abused, she ceases nesting. She doesn't feel like making things pretty because that ability is damaged. She becomes like a rose without any leaves or petals, just a stem with a few little thorns. Any man who grabs hold of her is going to get hurt. Many women are like this in the world.

They are hard and cold. They're not loving, kind and soft anymore. They don't want to cook anything or help anyone. The Men who come in close contact with them will endure pain from the association. This kind of a woman is super critical and always looking for any reason to be rid of the male. The mentality of women that men are only good for one thing is observed in wilted roses. This is a turn on the same line used to describe women by men who are broken bricks. When we try to explain things without truth you just hear people say it's the age and day we live in. They try to shrug off the pain of not being right by involvement in some other new thing that can occupy their muddled minds. Some of us may have had mothers or wives like this. It's sad, but these roses are wilted, abused or soiled because of unscrupulous men. In the bible it says; "Woe be unto evil men who prey upon weak willed women". They are not weak in the area of defining acceptability but are weak as far as being able to discern the con played by a man who represents in some fashion that he has his stuff together. A woman is easy prey for men because she is looking.

Scheming Men portray themselves to be what she is looking for. She may not even know what is wrong, because her hopes are that something good will come out of the situation. She knows she doesn't feel right, she doesn't feel beautiful anymore. She is depressed and feels raped. The beginnings of destruction are in place and without change her behavior will modify itself to accept momentary satisfaction. She will ultimately despise the man that is the source of her satisfaction. She may go another direction by completely rejecting all men. She is almost celibate but is still vulnerable to one last hope. She is excited about someone who appears to be safe and may let someone get close but fear keeps her heart locked. He could be all she has hoped for but he'll be rejected on the ground of being a man. Negative effect triumphs by keeping her from getting her dream. She will never accept a honest, trustable and dependable man. Both men and women are the losers in this old game which causes fear, mistrust and loneliness. Those who are innocent are often the ones to pay the price of this game.

The Great Spirit told Adam "I am going to make a present for you, a helper, someone you will love and cherish". This value has been so trampled on by society that roses don't even value themselves as roses. A rose seeks her value in jobs and with her career. She can run a company well using the gifts that the Great Spirit gave her to be a mother and wife. In opposition to our society, the value of a rose is in the characteristics she has to beautify the home, to raise children, to tend to and look after the needs of the family and to love and cherish her husband. Sarah, the wife of Abraham, said she thought of Abraham as her Lord and master. She respected him. She wouldn't have respected him if he did nothing that was respectable. He initiated good things in Sarah's life and therefore, she respected him.

13. FIXING BRICKS AND ROSES

Abused roses and broken bricks must realize that they are broken and abused. Books and psychologists can give insight and education but getting rid of negative behavior can only be accomplished by finding out why and when the negative behavior began. One needs to go to the root of the problem in order to understand how and why the problem exists. Sometimes the effort to find the beginning takes more than one attempt. Many times finding the source of one problem uncovers other problems. Some problems are linked to others. I call the problems negatives and negative behavior. Negative behavior is always accompanied with one or more negative spirits. Negative spirits do not like to be exposed. When you open their domain in you they will try to plant a thought in your mind to discredit the information you are finding. Once you find the truth and you believe it then the negative program and spirit has no place within you to stay. Believe me. Once you have started you will get quite an education. You'll be surprised and shocked. You will know, without a doubt, if you have succeeded in removing the negative program. The first area we need to deal with is admitting we have problems. Finding out we're not all right is emotionally traumatic and admitting it is even more trauma. We come to a point in our life when we realize that we don't know what is going on and we don't have a handle on everything. We find that we're pretty helpless when it comes to fixing our own lives and making things right. It's at this point when we say; "help me". Then the Great Spirit begins to help us by showing us where we are broken. The Great Spirit does not magically show us. Most often your mind becomes relaxed and you begin to see and understand in a way that seems completely natural. The amazing thing is that if it is so natural then why didn't it occur before now.

The first step to change is recognizing our negative behavior and finding it's root, the beginning point of it. We must also feel a release from whoever has offended us, used or abused us. Not being able to feel released from some one means you still have negative emotions linked to the situation. Vengeful anger and hate has a negative effect of it's own. Negative spirits and programs hang on to your emotional wounds. Healing of your wounds takes place in your heart when the negative program is exposed and you understand why it is there.

In order to go right to the root of our problem may require us to go back to a point in our childhood and find the event that first started our negative program. We have stored in our subconscious hard drive every emotionally stirring event of our lives. We often find abuse and the lack of love in our lives as children. Having an improper father and mother or not having a proper role model at all has a starting point in our lives. Now days many children don't have fathers. If they do have a father many of them are alcoholics, drug abusers, child molesters, or homosexuals. We will pattern our lives after an individual that reflects the environment that we are raised in.

The negative mistakes of our parents can carry on into the third and fourth generation. There is an unseen link from us to the negatives of our parents. It is not the child's fault. The children are neglected or abused by the parent and the negative from the parent becomes attached to the child. The children may go through life and in certain situations a negative spirit is able to pull on that attachment and cause them to do the very same thing their parents did to them. It is wonderful to find and to break those ties to our past and break the attachment to the negative behavior of our parents. Whatever your parents did you don't have to do. Truth sets us free. Truth helps us take responsibility for our lives and Truth removes us from the negative grasp. Truth can become the positive role model so many of us never had.

There are many negatives in the world that tear up the structure of bricks and roses. What the Great Spirit wants to do is deliver us from the negative that destroys our ability to be the way we are naturally made to be. We know that a broken brick is not solid and therefore cannot be used for any positive function. When the Great Spirit causes us to be transformed he places the strength back into us that is needed for us to stand strong in the worst situations. When the ground shakes or the mighty hurricane winds blow the brick must be strong enough to firmly stand still. In the story of the three little pigs one of them built a house out of straw, and one a house out of sticks. Those houses were blown down. But the house the third pig built out of bricks couldn't be blown down. The wolf in this story can be compared to an enemy negative spirit. The Great Spirit wants a man to be a tough brick so that when the enemy comes and huffs and puffs, he won't be able to blow us down. He won't be able to cave in the brick or damage the rose.

Broken bricks and wilted roses find themselves incapable of deterring from past negative programs, especially from sexual immorality. The Great Spirit begins by showing us what we think is love is really nothing more than fulfilling our own selfish motives. A silent cry exists, "won't you please love me"? This is a self-incriminating cry. What we misinterpret as being love is just emotion and selfish desire focused into and on ourselves. When the Great Spirit is finished in this area our love no longer focuses inward it focuses out. Then that person can be a help to others or be able to help the one they claim to love. This means doing for the other person what is right and not being concerned about our personal sexual desire. The Great Spirit does what is right for us even though we may fuss and complain or even threaten to no longer acknowledge Him. He's not worried because he knows we will love Him even more when we recognize the improvement He has made in our lives.

Broken bricks and soiled roses, in the state they are in, cannot be used for anything positive. When the Great Spirit restores us he can use us. Being used for positive changes is what every restored brick and rose desire. That desire is evidence of untainted love in us. The desire to be of use is because we have been released from negative programs and we are free from our own negative actions. The Great Spirit is totally capable of taking care of everything without help from us. He allows us to participate in His plan for our life out of His mercy and love for us. When positive changes occur in us we actually look different and feel different. It feels so good that you can't wipe the smile of off your face. I have a brother who has been going through the search, inspection, evaluation and change that happens when Truth exposes negative programs. My comment to him was "boy, you look different, you sound different. I like it"! Like I said, you can't wipe the smile off of his face. What does he want to do? He wants to continue finding negative programs in himself. He wants to restore positives in their place and then he wants to help others. He is excited; "do you know what this means"? "I'm going to be free".

The Great Spirit wants bricks to be and provide a safe place for women and children. He wants roses and children to be able to come under a brick's protection and not be abused. There isn't a single man that the Great Spirit doesn't want to be a solid brick and a safe place. There are roses searching for safety, yearning to be in a place safe from the world. The Great Spirit wants the brick to be a shield of protection.

A rose should be able to go to the brick with any pain ailing her and the brick should be able to comfort and console her. The rose is the emotional person in the family and is tied into the rest of the families' emotional needs. The brick is basically dense or fails to perceive the emotional needs. To stabilize herself and the family, the woman perceives the emotional needs with intuition and clues the brick in on a situation. Then the brick can deal solidly with whatever the situation requires. She feels good telling him and helping him and he feels good taking care of and protecting her and the family. History is a good text on human behavior. One can read age old documents and see the same human behaviors. The easy thing to perceive is the mistakes. Humans tend to exhibit great hind-sight. Even though we understand the mistakes and negative behavior of others we all seem to have a big problem relating the information to ourselves. When negative programs and negative spirits are out of the picture everything works as it was designed and all that are involved are very pleased and happy with the results.

14. BONDING

When a brick comes together sexually with a rose there is a bonding that takes place that no man can understand. This bonding is for the purpose and gift of becoming one. Sex before marriage breaks bricks and soils roses. The Great Spirit designed sex for union between committed partners. We call the committed union between a man and woman a "marriage". Negative spirits and programs misuse sex in order to destroy positive union. They establish distrust, lack of love and negative bonding between the rose and brick. Truth tells us that there is a big difference between love and lust.

Man has developed all kinds and forms of birth control. The unspoken communication is saying to women that any sexual activity is ok. We can see to it that you can be active sexually and not have to get pregnant. This confirms in most people's minds that the only deterrent to sexual activity is pregnancy. We have all types of contraceptives and abortion is legal. This tells women there is no reason why you shouldn't be involved sexually. To men it says you don't have to be responsible for what you do. Biblically speaking, the Great Spirit says that whatever a man touches sexually, he becomes one with. Knowing the positive program for men, we know that he is responsible for it. Even if a man is sexually in contact with a prostitute he becomes one with her. The spiritual part of this action is brought out when the Apostle Paul said there is a bonding that takes place between a man and woman that men and women do not understand. This is a profound mystery to men and women. It's profound and mysterious because we can't see it. A male-female bond can be strengthened through commitment, love and respect. The bonding that occurs between a man and a woman is strengthened by sexual union between the two of them. Sexual bonding is positive when it occurs in a committed relationship, a marriage. A sad thing is if there is no commitment bonding still occurs. These facts cause me to think about some women that I have known. These particular women are unable to bond to any man in a committed relationship because they are already bonded to many different men. You can take a strip of tape off the roll and stick it most anything. Then pull the tape and stick it to something else. Do this a few times and you will find that pretty soon that piece of tape will not stick any more. Each time it was stuck to something different the tape lost a little bit of ability to stick. The Great Spirit made this bonding mechanism so there would be something to hold us together when everything isn't right. Like when the husband has had a hard day at the office and comes home grouchy. The wife has had a bad time with the kids throughout the day. When he comes home he feels disenchanted and separated from his family. There is a link that keeps them together. The link that holds them together is the invisible bond that the Great Spirit built into their lives through their sexual contact with each other. Does the Great Spirit want sexual contact, the strong bonding of it outside of marriage? No! He would not because we haven't made the decision or the commitment to be a responsible safe place for that person. What happens through negative sexual contact is we begin bonding ourselves to a negative. I don't care who taught you math but I know that two negatives never add up to a positive. The only thing that you will get is more negative.

With sexual immorality the positive bonding mechanism begins to break. Without the commitment of marriage, sexual activity produces a back taste feeling of pain and remorse. The rose will feel her petals and leaves being stripped off and she will cry "why do I feel this way"? She initially thinks sexual contact is a wonderful and beautiful experience but when it's over she doesn't feel so wonderful or beautiful. The rose feels violated and hurt but doesn't understand why. She doesn't trust this man now because he has violated her and has proven to her that he is unsafe for her. If the relationship continues and they become married, it may take years to replace the precious gift of trust and safety that the Great Spirit intended to be there. In her subconscious mind this brick has violated her and he is capable of violating someone else.

It shows her that he is not in control of his sexuality. His sexuality is in control of him.

There doesn't seem to be a conscience in a man when he is sexually aroused. The bonding mechanism that the Great Spirit meant for good is being used for bad. A negative spirit's chief goal is to destroy what the Great Spirit made for good by making it negative. The negative takes a toll on the rose first because she is the beautiful part of the positive. She feels dirty at first and becomes an emotional wreck by deeply involving herself in it. When she continues to involve herself in immorality she becomes hard and callused to true emotion and love. For her there is no longer any love in sexuality. It becomes simply "sex". This is more of negative programming because the Great Spirit never intended for sexuality to create love. He intended love and commitment to cause sexuality. Where there is marriage and commitment, sexuality is the icing on the cake and a bonding link holding the two together.

Sexual immorality causes men to lose value for the Great Spirit gift. They tarnish and strip the petals off the rose. Then the man looks at her and thinks she is not beautiful anymore. The man is responsible for the actions that cause her to appear ugly. Scripture says woe unto those who prey upon weak willed women. In our language it would be "if you mess around with that tramp your going to be sorry""!

In sexual immorality the linking mechanism is broken and no longer able to hold. There is no stick power in the adhesive. It is worn away, dirty, and misused. The same thing happens in casual sexual contact. What the Great Spirit designed to hold us together, when used for the wrong purpose, can't stick. This is another reason why divorce is so rampant in the world. Five out of ten marriages result in divorce. Out of the five that result in divorces usually several of them have already been married and divorced two or more times. People are accepting divorce as a norm in life. There was a time when divorce was not acceptable.

In our era everyone is doing it and they see nothing wrong with it. If you evaluate the situation and add a dab of truth you will agree that there is definitely something wrong. It's time we began seeking the truth and quit hiding in lies. Sometimes I get so upset with humanity that I ask, "isn't there something else I could be"? I don't want to be a human. Humans are too damn stupid!

A friend recently told me he was having a sexual relationship with a lady he was not married to. He tried justifying it by saying that "God" made him with sexuality so "God" made him act on it and therefore it's okay. He also said he was feeling conviction and wanted to know why. The Great Spirit did not intend what he made for positive to be used for negative. The Great Spirit is not the author of negative. In the Old Testament the Great Spirit had severe consequences for sexual immorality. At that time immorality could be death for a brick, a rose or both. They could be stoned at the city wall. The Great Spirit says we don't live by the law the law lives in us. Truth puts the law in us through a positive spirit. Even today, our negative actions have unavoidable "effect".

The Great Spirit wants us to straighten our lives out and be responsible. He says a man should discipline himself. The Apostle Paul said that he beat the flesh daily. What he was saying is he had the same desires we have but that he disciplined himself. He put down negative desire.

Broken bricks and wilted roses are unable to love and be truly loved, although they want to. Because of the society we live in, sexuality is often mistaken for love. This is a deviant coping mechanism. We feel worse than before because we keep violating ourselves. The result is unresolved pain and anguish that can cause divorce. It's the simple principle of "cause and effect". If its not the man stripping the rose of its beauty, then it's society stripping the rose and leaving her with just thorns. Society tries to stuff bricks and roses together when no commitment exists. Then what happens is the two become so disgusted with each other they turn outside of the marriage to find some other victim. Some times they look to a person of the same sex believing and hoping they will be understood. You have broken bricks with broken bricks and violated roses with stripped and violated roses. The blind trying to lead the blind. This results in a deepening of the attached negative behavior which in turn begins telling you that its okay if you have these feelings towards your partner of the same sex. (Romans 1:27,28 Leviticus 18:22, 20:13). Biblically speaking, the Great Spirit never made us to be this way. It is a violation of the way we were made.

Negative programs and negative spirits are victorious when they have perverted what the Great Spirit made for good. The book of Malachi 4:25 says the Great Spirit wishes men would return to the wife of their youth. That in doing so they become the godly offspring. Some people believe this means they will create godly offspring, children. It really means they become godly offspring when two come together as one flesh, the way the Great Spirit made them to be. This one flesh is the godly offspring. A brick will leave his mother and father and cleave unto his rose and the two become one flesh. When a brick and rose come together as one they are complete like the Great Spirit is complete.

The world does everything it can to separate bricks and roses. It makes the rose accept being alone and independent, seeking her okay in life from her career. Then the world takes the brick and makes him believe he must be separate doing his own thing. The Great Spirit says no! These two should become one flesh and have no division.

Negative does the same thing with the drug addict and alcoholic. The high of the drugs and alcohol do not last and the addict must keep doing them over and over again to keep them selves in the euphoric state that they crave. The physical pleasure of sexual activity outside of marriage is momentary and once it is gone the guilt, conviction and destruction set in. People wonder why they feel so used and taken advantage of. The reason is they have just abused and mistreated something that the Great Spirit made for good. If you buy a new pair of shoes and the first time you wear them you scuff up the toes you are never going to be able to fix the damage. You may feel bad and wish that you had not damaged them but to get the use out of them you will just have to get used to wearing them in the condition they are in.

15. BRICK AND ROSE RESPONSIBILITIES

Our main responsibility is each other and the children in our care. (Ephesians. 5:19-33) With the information that I have provided I hope that we can all add up the responsibilities. The Brick is a protector and a provider. He also needs to be a good listener. The Rose is a mother. It is only through her that the human species continues. She is also a helper. To put it very simple it takes the two of them to make life exist. Everything else revolves around that.

People like to listen to what a professional has to say about any particular issue. I have five daughters and have been married four times. I should have enough experience with male-female relationships to be considered a professional. Even with sufficient experience, it wasn't until I realized that I didn't know that I questioned myself and started seeking answers. At the time of completing this manuscript my youngest daughter is three years old and my eldest is twenty seven. My youngest likes to change clothes several times a day. She mothers everything including all animals that allow her the opportunity. She likes to help her mother cook. She also likes to help her dad irrigate the fields. What she likes most is riding the horses. She likes to participate in the kids rodeos that are held during the summer months. In one event she unties the ribbon from a goats tail but her favorite is riding the horse through poles and barrels even though someone is leading the horse. With the knowledge I have acquired, I definitely know that she's a girl.

It is my goal to do everything I can to remove all negative programs and negative spirits from myself. I hope that this book has enlightened you to the point that you become a seeker of truth. Understanding and accepting truth will make a change in you. You'll be surprised.

ABOUT THE AUTHOR

Crae Forrest Hancock

Born: October 3 1948 the oldest of five children

Place of birth: Roosevelt, Utah

Schools: Grade schools and High school diploma at Bingham High in Cooperton, Utah

Ricks College in Rexburg, Idaho 1 year

Brigham Young University, Provo, Utah 2 years

Major: Public Relations and Advertising with Minor in Fine Arts

Religion: None

Marriage: Yes

Children: Yes, five girls and one boy

Languages: English, speak Finnish and some
                   Jewish

Occupation: General   Contractor   and
                   certified   designer   and
                   installer of Septic systems

Pilot: Hold Private Pilot Certificate
                   with   sign   off   in Aerobatics,
                   High   performance, Raised   gear
                   and Tail wheel

Interests: Soft ball, Basketball, Horses,
                   Flying,   Boating,   Research,
                   Writing and Art

www.ingramcontent.com/pod-product-compliance
Lightning Source LLC
Chambersburg PA
CBHW022245290526
45785CB00015B/197